Copyright
for Teachers
and Librarians

Rebecca P. Butler

Neal-Schuman Publishers, Inc.

New York   London

Published by Neal-Schuman Publishers, Inc.
100 William Street
New York, NY 10038

Printed and bound in the United States of America

The paper used in this publication meets the minimum requirements of American National Standard for Information Sciences—Permanence of Paper for Printed Library Materials. ANSI Z39.48-1992.○

PLEASE READ THIS:
We have done our best to give you useful and accurate information on copyright law. But please be aware that laws and precedents are constantly changing and are subject to different interpretations. The information presented here does not substitute for the advice of an attorney. You have the responsibility to check all material you read here before relying on it. Of necessity, neither Neal-Schuman nor the author makes any warranties concerning the information in this book or the use to which it is put.

"This publication is designed to provide accurate and authoritative information in regard to the subject matter covered. It is sold with the understanding that the publisher is not engaged in rendering legal, accounting or other professional service. If legal advice or other expert assistance is required, the services of a competent professional person should be sought." *From a Declaration of Principles adopted jointly by a Committee of the American Bar Association and a Committee of Publishers.*

Library of Congress Cataloging-in-Publication Data

Butler, Rebecca P.
  Copyright for teachers and librarians / Rebecca P. Butler.
    p. cm.
  Includes bibliographical references and index.
  ISBN 1-55570-500-6 (alk. paper)
  1. Copyright—United States. 2. Fair use (Copyright)—United States.
  3. Teachers—Legal status, laws, etc.—United States. I. Title.
  KF2995.B88 2004
  346.7304'82—dc22
                                                            2004046013

To my two biggest supporters, my husband, Tom,
and my son, Benjamin. Thank you for always being there!

Contents

List of Figures
and Flow Charts

Preface

Over the past eight years, I have conducted a series of copyright workshops, classes, and presentations for teachers, school library media specialists, public and academic librarians, technology coordinators, school administrators, higher education students, and other interested parties. They came to these sessions for much the same reason that you picked up this book—they realized the importance and complexity of copyright issues in the classroom setting and wanted help. *Copyright for Teachers and Librarians* is largely based on the questions and concerns raised by those in my workshops and classes, so it speaks to the needs of educators and recognizes how copyright fits into your professional lives.

Copyright for Teachers and Librarians is, first and foremost, a handbook on copyright law for teachers, school library media specialists, technology coordinators, administrators, and others who work with students in the K–12 environment. In addition, the information included in this book can be used by, or taught to, elementary, middle school, and secondary school students. I have chosen to use realistic examples with interpretations of the law from copyright experts in the field. Although reading and interpreting the United States Copyright Law (Public Law 94–553) for oneself would be one approach, teachers and librarians may choose to use the interpretations from copyright experts given in the book so that they don't have to wade through the law on their own. Because copyright law leaves some gray areas, there may be more than one interpretation to any one question. Since that is the case, I have chosen to give the readers the answer I consider most practical and most applicable in a K–12 school setting. For other concerns, or for your further education, you may refer to the law itself, at www.copyright.gov/title17/.

This book is divided into two practical and necessary parts. Part I introduces the general concepts associated with copyright law. Part II describes the specific applications of copyright law as they affect nine different formats. It is important to use and understand both parts of this book, as they really do speak to each other. Knowing the general concepts will help your understanding and use of the specific applications. In the same way, knowing how copyright applies to your position in education will help you better understand and read the copyright legislation and literature you encounter in your day-to-day work. While you may refer to the chapters of part II more frequently than part I, you won't understand the information of part II without having read part I.

Through the five chapters of part I, readers will develop a basic knowledge of the language and provisions of copyright law. Chapter One, "Introduction to Copyright Law: What Is Copyright?" provides a basic explanation of copyright, a history of legislation, its importance, how it affects media, and the policies and ethics associated with copyrighted materials. Chapter Two, "Fair Use: When Do You Need to Ask for Permission?" introduces readers to four factors of fair use that will help them make the best decisions for using materials and seeking written permissions. This chapter also provides guidelines for the popular educational multimedia materials teachers and librarians often use. Chapter Three, "Public Domain: Is There Such a Thing as Free Material?" answers questions about one of the most speculated on aspects of copyright—public domain materials. This chapter will explain public domain, including how something becomes public domain, what media are public domain, the relation of government documents and public domain, and how you can identify works in the public domain. Chapter Four, "Obtaining Permission: How Can You Legally Obtain Use of Works?" gets to the core and function of this book. This chapter will outline permissions (what are they and how they work) and help you understand their relationship to clearinghouses and licenses. This chapter also explains how to write a permissions letter, what goes in it, and an example of an effective letter. Chapter Five, "Other Important Copyright Issues: What Other Copyright Issues Do You Need to Know About?" explains some of the remaining issues including international copyright law, plagiarism and citation, and violations and penalties.

Chapters Six through Twelve in part II, cover the specific applications of copyright law to Internet, videos, CDs, DVDs, television, computer software, music and audio, multimedia, and print works. Although teachers and librarians are familiar with terms such as "media" and "mediums," for the purpose of this book, I have chosen to use the word "work" to represent these items as it is the more common term used with copyright law. Each chapter explains fair use, public domain, documentation and licenses, permissions, creation and ownership, violations and penalties, international copyright law, and avoiding copyright problems as they relate to the specific works. These are chapters that you can consult as the issues arise or read over to become more familiar with the formats you use most often. Chapter Thirteen, "Distance Learning and Copyright Law: Is This Different from Appling Copyright Law in a Face-to-Face Classroom?" discusses the TEACH Act and how it relates to this new and upcoming material. Chapter Fourteen, "Conclusion: What Does All of This Mean for K–12 Educators?" brings it all together and provides some last-minute advice for not running into problems, how to deal with pressure to break the law, and how and why to teach students and faculty the importance of copyright law.

Copyright law is one of those things that is rarely emphasized in library school or elementary education programs. It is something that you have probably always been aware of, but that perhaps you have never examined closely. The truth is that copyright is an everyday part of your function as a teacher or librarian, and it requires your full attention and knowledge. This guide is meant to be a quick and thorough education in the implications of copyright on K–12 education. I have answered many of the common questions I have encountered in my workshops while still expanding and fleshing out this source so that it anticipates even the questions that were not asked. In truth, copyright can be a help rather than a hindrance to the education of our youth, but it is necessary to be aware of the various facets of copyright and use them to your own and your students' advantage.

Acknowledgments

I would like to thank those K–12 teachers, school librarians, technology coordinators, and public librarians whose demand for information on copyright in a "non-legalese" manner has culminated in this book. Additionally, I would like to thank my instructional technology students, other interested master's and doctoral students, graduate assistants, and interested faculty colleagues at Northern Illinois University and East Tennessee State University who have participated in my copyright classes and workshops over the past ten years and asked insightful questions on the subject. This book would also not be possible without the support of Debbie Abilock, editor of *Knowledge Quest,* the journal of the American Association of School Librarians, who first asked me to write a copyright column. I would also like to thank Charles Harmon and Michael Kelley of Neal-Schuman Publishers: Charles, who "discovered" me via *Knowledge Quest,* and Michael, my editor, who has provided much guidance and support in the writing of this, my first book. In addition, I would like to thank Eileen Fitzsimons, copy editor extraordinaire. Next, I wish to express my appreciation for the support of family and friends whose kind words and help—when they were most needed—kept me on track. Thanks for taking time out of your busy lives when I needed it most! Lastly, I wish to thank my husband, Tom, and my son, Benjamin, who read over drafts, made comments, and helped create flow charts. Thank you all! This book is for you!

Part I

Essential Concepts of Copyright Law

Chapter One

Introduction to Copyright Law: What Is Copyright?

INTRODUCTION

Copyright is a very muddy area of law with lots of interpretations. It is especially of concern in a K-12 educational setting, where teachers, administrators, library media specialists, technology coordinators, students, and others may think, "We're a school. We can copy all we want, because it's for education." If the copyright owner has granted consent for use of his or her work, then there is no problem. Frequently, however, the dilemma is that the borrower does not have the time or inclination (or is unable) to locate the owner in order to ask for the needed permission.

Often, those of us in schools think we will not get caught if we borrow without obtaining permission from the work's owner. After all, we do not do it all the time, and who has really heard of copyright police? There is also the opposite approach, when a school administrator may demand that absolutely *no* copying occur in his or her school building. Here, the misconception is that *all* copying is illegal. Actually, the answer lies somewhere in between. As teachers and librarians, we deal with communication technologies in a wide variety of formats, from books to videos to the Internet. We are usually busy and often searching for something to use at the last minute. Borrowing a few pages out of a textbook for an English class to take home over the weekend, copying another piece of music for the drum section, or using a popular song for a cheerleading video may seem the easiest way to go. After all, who is going to know? That the owner of the copyrighted work may lose money or control over his or her product is not our concern. Below are some of the questions that we *should* ask as we go about our daily responsibilities as educators.

Do you need special permission from Internet authors to use their works? Can you print anything you want off a CD-ROM? Is it okay to copy a television program and use it in your classroom? Legally, is it possible to show a video or DVD rented from a video store in homeroom? Can you change a digitized image enough so that using it is not copyright infringement? Is it possible to legally retain students' completed assignments to use in future classes or to show as "best examples"? If you want to copy a magazine article 30 times for a class reading assignment, can you do this under copyright law? K-12 educators often ask such questions as they develop curriculum, prepare lessons, and otherwise go about their daily teaching duties. All of these questions deal with copyright, perhaps the most well known of our intellectual property rights.[1] They will be covered in the next few chapters along with other copyright topics.

As you use this book, please note that there are three similar terms: U.S. Code, U.S. Copyright Law, and the U.S. Copyright Act. Although they are all related, each one is different. The *U.S. Code* "is the codification by subject matter of the general and permanent laws of the United States. It is divided by broad subjects into 50 titles and published by the Office of the Law Revision Counsel of the U.S. House of Representatives" (U.S. Code, 2003, 1). One part of the U.S. Code is Title 17. Chapters 1–8 and 10–12 of Title 17 contain the *United States Copyright Law.*[2] This is the U.S. law that is concerned with copyright and, thus, the one we use in this book to interpret our copyright questions. The *Copyright Act* is part of the U.S. Copyright Law. Passed in 1976, the Copyright Act "provides the basic framework for the current copyright law . . ." (U.S. Copyright Law, 2002, 1). The complete Copyright Law is available in a variety of places, including the Copyright office's Web site <www.copyright.gov>.

COPYRIGHT DEFINED AND EXPLAINED

Below is a brief definition of copyright and what it means to those of us in elementary, middle, and secondary schools.

Definition

"Copyright is a statutory privilege extended to creators of works that are fixed in a tangible medium of expression" (Bruwelheide, 1995, 4). Owners of copyrighted works have the exclusive right, by law, to

---

Figure 1-1
Works That Can Be Copyrighted

Print
Books
Newspapers
Articles
Newsletters
Letters
Poems
Sheet Music
Plays and Musicals
Other Print Works

Nonprint
Videos
DVDs
CD-ROMs
Computer Software
Audio Recordings

Nonprint *(continued)*
Multimedia
Photographs
Television Programs
Modern Dance and Other Public
    Performances
Statues
Paintings
Other Nonprint Works

Internet
Web Pages
E-mails
Digitized Graphics, Movies, and Advertisements
Other Digitized Works Available on
    the World Wide Web

- reproduce or copy,
- distribute,
- publicly perform,
- publicly display, and
- create derivatives.

Copyright law violations occur when someone other than the owner attempts to use works in one of the manners described above (Butler, 2000).

Things That Can Be Copyrighted

Almost anything originally created is copyrightable.[3] Figure 1-1 lists examples of works that can be copyrighted.

Automatic Copyright

Under current copyright law, almost anything a person creates is automatically copyrighted, whether it is officially registered or not. Thus, every e-mail you send, every paper you write, every digital picture you take is protected. What this means for K-12 educators is that a high school coach who creates a Web site to supplement football practice, a student who writes an original paper on John Brown, and a fifth-grade teacher who films a video of his or her students' art work have all created copyrightable works. If you like, you may put a © on everything you or your students create. This shows those who view/listen/use your work that it is copyrighted, whether officially registered with the U.S. Copyright Office or not. (Official registration of copyright is addressed later in this chapter.) Remember: in the instance of a lawsuit, those items registered with the U.S. Copyright Office have a stronger chance of winning than do those that have only been "unofficially" copyrighted (Bruwelheide, 1995).

Who Owns Copyrights?

Usually the person who creates a work owns the copyright; for example, a student who burns a CD-ROM of a series of stories that he has written for English class would probably own the rights to his stories. However, it is possible for individuals or companies to own works they did not create. This can occur in one of two ways. The first is when the creator transfers or assigns the copyright to a third party. Thus, it is possible for a technology coordinator to create a Web page about child care among penguins on his or her own time and sell the copyright to an educational Internet company. The second way is "work for hire." This is when work, created by an individual, is considered the property of the organization that hired him or her to do the work (Butler, 2002a). For example, a school-library media specialist uses his free period for several weeks to write up a collection-development policy. He was asked to create this policy by the school superintendent, he is doing it on school time, and he uses a school computer. Such a situation is usually considered "work for hire." Another example is if a mathematics teacher, at home, creates a piece of math software for an educational software company. If she signs a contract with the company stating that it is "work for hire," the teacher does not own what she has created. The teacher is paid a fee by the software company, which then copyrights the software.

Derivative Works

Derivative works are items created by changing an already existing work. The extent of change to the work can be slight, moderate, or a great deal. Take a graphic of an elephant, for example. A Web designer has created an elephant for her Web site. A school student finds the elephant graphic and borrows it, adding a red hat to its head. The elephant with a red hat is an example of a derivative work. Another example of a derivative work is when an elementary school media specialist takes a popular rap song and changes the words to fit a fourth-grade unit on the Dewey Decimal Classification System. When works are changed some-what—but not completely—a derivative work is the result. When derivative works are created from copyrighted works, without the proper permissions or licenses, this is an infringement of copyright law.

HISTORY OF COPYRIGHT

Those who do not teach history might wonder, "Why is the history of copyright important to my students and me?" Most teachers and librarians have their eyes to the future, to new technologies and how to use them in the classroom. As will be seen from the discussion below, however, while copyright is often seen as a relatively new concern, especially with new technologies, it has, in fact, been around for some time. Understanding where it has been before can help with thinking about where it will go in the future. "One way we have of sensing the future is to look back into the past" (Saltrick, 1995, 1).

Copyright in the United States is greatly influenced by English common law. For example, the Statute of Anne of 1710, noted as the beginning of contemporary copyright law, provided for protecting authors' literary property for a limited number of years (Tryon, 1994). Notions of copyright in the future United States are seen as early as 1672, when bookseller John Usher's petition to the General Court of the Massachusetts Bay Colony resulted in a private copyright for his revised edition of *The General Laws and Liberties of the Massachusetts Colony* (Bettig, 1996; U.S. Library of Congress, 1963). About 100 years later, such prominent citizens of the fledging United States as Noah Webster and Thomas Paine worked to promote state copyright law.[4] The first federal copyright law was signed in 1790 by President George Washington. Congress was given the power to "promote the progress of science and useful arts, by securing for limited times to authors and inventors the exclusive right to their respective writings and discoveries" (U.S. Const., art. I sec. 8). This law was expanded and revised in 1831, 1879, 1909, 1976, and 1998. It is the basis of intellectual property rights in our country today, and continues to be expanded and revised. At any given point in time, a number of bills dealing in some way with copyright sit in our nation's House and Senate awaiting action (Butler, 2003). Many new bills cover electronic works, such as the Internet, television broadcasting, DVDs, and computer software. Indeed in the new millennium, ". . . one of the primary reasons for copyright law is . . . the protection of the owners and creators to earn money and recognition for those things that they own or create" (Butler, 2003, 39).

WHY COPYRIGHT LAW IS IMPORTANT

Copyright is important in that it protects creators' and owners' rights to their works. Copyright legislation grants the owner the "exclusive right to reproduce, prepare derivative works, distribute, perform and display the work publicly. Exclusive means only the creator of such work, not anybody who has access to it and decides to grab it" (Whatiscopyright.org, 2003, 8). However, copyright law also helps the user of the work, in that the owners' rights are limited (see chapters 2 and 3). As such, this law actually represents both the owners and the users of works.

It is helpful here to look briefly at owners and users of works—usually two distinctive groups. Owners are those individuals or groups who either created a work or obtained the copyright for it. Usually, owners are looking for assurance that the rights they own are not being infringed upon. Users of works are those individuals or groups who wish to borrow all or part of a work for their own employ. For example, suppose you are a teacher and you wish to borrow a series of activities from a reading workbook for use with your sixth-grade class. If you plan to photocopy these activities and share them with colleagues, it is very possible that you would be violating the rights of those who own the copyright to the reading activities. These two distinct groups are what keep the issue of copyright going, year after year, generation after generation. Next, you will learn how to obtain an official copyright for a work that you have created.

HOW TO COPYRIGHT WORKS[5]

Usually when you think of copyright, you think in terms of how much you can borrow without getting permission from the owner or creator of the book, video, audio-tape, Web page, or whatever it is that you want to copy. However, look at this subject from a different approach—how you can officially register something you have created with the U.S. Copyright Office.

Assume that you are a retired teacher with a hobby in astronomy. As a former middle school teacher, you have decided to try your hand at creating units on astronomy for middle school students. You have written a number of units, created on your own time, at home, with your own software and computer. These have not been used in the classroom. You compile the units into manuscript form, with the idea that perhaps an educational publishing firm would be interested in them. Before you send them out for review, you would like to obtain official copyright registration for your work. How do you go about doing this?

Contacting the Copyright Office

Your first step is to contact the U.S. Copyright Office at the Library of Congress. They can be reached by phone, mail, or over the Internet. If you are contacting them by phone or mail, tell them that you want to register your manuscript with their office, and they will send you the materials you need. All forms and application instructions, as well as other copyright information, are also available on the Web at www.loc.gov/copyright. (You will need Adobe Acrobat Reader in order to view and print these materials.)

What Can Be Registered and What Forms Do You Need to Do So?

Be aware that any kind of work that can be copyrighted can be registered with the U.S. Copyright Office. Form TX and short Form TX (both of which can be used to register the manuscript example) are used with either published or unpublished "nondramatic literary works," including "fiction, nonfiction, poetry, textbooks, reference works, directories, catalogs, advertising copy, compilations of information, and computer programs" (U.S. Copyright Office, 2004). Other works that can be assigned copyright registration include lyrics, music, plays, videos, scripts, pantomimes, choreography, sound recordings, cartoons, comic strips, photographs, architectural works, games, multimedia works, and recipes.

Note that there are some works that cannot be registered by the Copyright Office. Such works include those protected by another intellectual property, such as a patent or those that are not entitled to protection, for example works that are not set in a fixed form (Torrans, 2003). In addition, other works that cannot be copyrighted include ideas, methods, blank forms, names, titles, slogans, short phrases and

> works that consist entirely of information that is common property and contain(ing) no original authorship. . . . Among these are "standard calendars, height and weight charts, tape measures and rules, and lists of tables taken from public documents or other common sources . . . mere listings of ingredients or contents, procedures, systems, processes, concepts, principles, discoveries, or devices" (Torrans, 40).

The following are the long and short registration forms for published and unpublished works:

- literary works, Forms TX
- periodicals and serials, Forms SE
- performing arts, Forms PA
- sound recordings, Forms SR

- visual arts, Forms VA
- copyright renewal, Form RE

Information requested on the forms, which must be completed for each item, comprise title, name and address of author, name and address of owner, year of creation, publication date (if applicable), type of authorship (Is the item text only, text and illustrations, etc.?), author signature, name and address of permission contact person, and where the copyright certificate is to be mailed (U.S. Copyright Office, 2004).

Registering Your Work

To register your work, you will need to do the following:

1. Obtain the necessary forms. (If you are the only author or copyright owner, the work is not made for hire, and it is completely new, then you may use the short form version of each application, available for most works.)
2. Complete the appropriate application (form).
3. Send a nonrefundable filing fee. (Check with the U.S. Copyright Office for fee amount. As of December 5, 2003, it was $30.00 [U.S. Copyright Office, 2004].)
4. Attach 1 or 2 non-returnable copies of the work. (This will vary, depending on whether your work is published or unpublished and on whether it was published in the United States or another country. The number of copies needed will be stated in the information you receive from the Copyright Office. Read this information carefully.) For the purposes of the example given, because your work was created in the U.S. and is presently unpublished, one copy is enough. Send these three items in the same envelope or package back to the U.S. Copyright Office in the Library of Congress.

When Does Your Work Receive Copyright Registration?

"A copyright registration is effective on the date of receipt in the Copyright Office of all required elements in acceptable form, regardless of the length of time it takes to process the application and mail the certificate of registration" (U.S. Copyright Office, 2004). Therefore, if your work can be registered for copyright protection, it will be protected immediately upon being received by the U.S. Copyright Office.

When Will You Find Out If Your Work Received Copyright Registration?

Normally, the person(s) requesting copyright registration will not receive any communication from the U.S. Copyright Office until about eight months after submission of the materials. At that time, you should either receive a certificate of registration or a letter explaining why your request has been rejected. You may also receive a call from an employee of the Copyright Office if more information is needed.

For our unpublished manuscript example (units for teaching astronomy to middle school students), registering the medium in the Copyright Office would be a relatively simple matter. You would need to fill out Short Form TX and mail it along with a copy of your unpublished manuscript and a check for $30.00. Your manuscript receives copyright registration no later than the time it took to mail the materials to the Copyright Office, and in approximately eight months, the official copyright registration should be sent to you. Congratulations! You now own a piece of work registered by the U.S. Copyright Office, Library of Congress!

U.S. Copyright Office Contact Information

Library of Congress
Copyright Office
101 Independence Avenue, S.E.
Washington, D.C. 20559-6000
(202) 707-3000
TTY(202) 707-6737
Internet: www.loc.gov/copyright

CONCLUSION: IF YOU WERE TO ASK EVERYONE IN THE ROOM WHO HAS VIOLATED COPYRIGHT LAW TO STAND, WOULD THE WHOLE ROOM STAND UP?

Were you to ask this question at a teachers' meeting in your school district, and complete honesty were required, then, yes, undoubtedly the whole room would stand. Answering the following questions will give you an idea as to why. In the past few years, have you or someone you know

- loaded a piece of computer software that a student brought in onto more than one classroom computer at the same time (without reading the documentation, which states that such use is illegal)?
- taken a boom box and taped a music CD to cassette tapes, so that students could listen to it in small groups with classroom audio-cassette recorders?
- "borrowed" liberally from a Web page that you liked to create one of your own?

- showed a personal video during recess on a rainy day?
- copied an extra script of a play for the new student director?
- made extra copies of a workbook page because the school didn't purchase a workbook for every student in the class?
- re-written the words to a popular song to teach the Dewey Decimal System to your third graders?
- used a color copier to copy all the pages of a picture book, which you then put up on a bulletin board?

The list goes on and on. Without proper permissions or other exemptions, all of these can be considered copyright infringement. Indeed, abuse of U.S. copyright law probably occurs every day in our schools. Be aware that even *you* might be caught! Now, continue on to chapter 2, for a discussion of fair use, one of the primary points of interest under copyright law.

END NOTES

1. Patents, trademarks, brand names, and copyrights are all examples of intellectual property. It . . . "may not be something you can put your arms around, but it exists and it has value" (Besenjak, 1997, 18–19).
2. "Chapters 9 and 13 of title 17 contain statutory design protection that is independent of copyright protection" (U.S. Copyright Law, 2002, 1).
3. The perception of an original work is that it "reflects the personality of the maker" (Ploman and Hamilton, 1980, 31). Thus, two different people may write stories about voice classes at the Peking Opera School, and both stories can be copyrighted—assuming that each story is sufficiently unique. Because this can be confusing, sometimes courts make the decision as to whether or not a work is "truly" an original (Ploman and Hamilton, 1980).
4. In the 1780s, state copyright laws were passed by all 13 original colonies as a result of Noah Webster's work to protect his writings. This was necessary because the Articles of Confederation did not provide federal copyright protection (Bettig, 1996; Peterson, 2003).
5. This section of chapter 1 is based in large part on an article that was first published as Butler, Rebecca P. 2002b. "How to Register Your Work with the U.S. Copyright Office." *Knowledge Quest* 30, no. 5 (May/June): 47–48.

REFERENCES

Besenjak, Cheryl. 1997. *Copyright Plain & Simple.* Franklin Lakes, NJ: Career Press.

Bettig, Ronald V. 1996. *Copyrighting Culture: The Political Economy of Intellectual Property.* Boulder, CO: Westview Press.

Bruwelheide, Janis H. 1995. *The Copyright Primer for Librarians and Educators.* 2nd ed. Chicago: American Library Association.

Butler, Rebecca P. 2000. "Copyright as a Social Responsibility—Don't Shoot the Messenger." *Knowledge Quest* 29, no. 2 (November/December): 48–49.

———. 2002a. "Copyright and Electronic Media in K-12 Education." Workshop for Improving Learning for All Students through Technology [grant], San Marcos, CA, February 20.

———. 2002b. "How to Register Your Work with the U.S. Copyright Office." *Knowledge Quest* 30, no. 5 (May/June): 47–48.

———. 2003. "Copyright Law in the United States . . . And How It Got That Way." *Knowledge Quest* 31, no. 4 (March/April): 39–40.

Peterson, Dennis L. "The Enduring Legacy of Noah Webster." *Homeschooling Today Magazine* (January/February 2003). Available: www.homeschoolingtoday.com/Articles/DPJF03.htm (accessed June 2, 2004).

Ploman, Edward W., and L. Clark Hamilton. 1980. *Copyright: Intellectual Property in the Information Age.* Boston: Routledge and Kegan Paul.

Saltrick, Susan. 1995. "The Pearl of Great Price: Copyright and Authorship from the Middle Ages to the Digital Age." *Educom Review* 30, no. 3 (May/June): 44–46.

Torrans, Lee Ann. 2003. *Law for K-12 Libraries and Librarians.* Westport, CT: Libraries Unlimited.

Tryon, Jonathan S. 1994. *The Librarian's Legal Companion.* New York: G. K. Hall.

U.S. Code. 2003. "Office of the Law Revision Counsel of the U.S. House of Representatives." (December). Available through GPO Access at www.gpoaccess.gov/uscode/ (accessed June 9, 2004).

U.S. Copyright Law. 1976. Public Law 94-553.

———. 2002. Preface [to Public Law 94-553 (October 19, 1976) and amendments]. Available: www.copyright.gov/title 17/preface.pdf (accessed June 12, 2004).

U.S. Copyright Office, Library of Congress. 1963. *Copyright Enactments.* Washington, D.C.: Government Printing Office.

————. 2004. Washington, DC: Library of Congress. (April). Available: www.loc.gov/copyright (accessed June 2, 2004).

Whatiscopyright.org. 2003. "What Is Copyright Protection?" Austin, TX: (January). Available: www.whatiscopyright.org/ (accessed June 2, 2004).

Chapter Two

Fair Use: When Do You Need to Ask for Permission?

FAIR USE DEFINED AND EXPLAINED

Probably one of the handiest and yet most easily misinterpreted copyright principle deals with fair use. Fair use "limits copyright holders' exclusive rights" (Butler, 2001a, 35). There are four fair use factors: "(1) the purpose and character of the use, including whether such use is of a commercial nature or is for nonprofit educational purposes; (2) the nature of the copyrighted work; (3) the amount and substantiality of the portion used in relation to the copyrighted work as a whole; and (4) the effect of the use upon the potential market for or value of the copyrighted work" (Lawrence and Timberg, 1989, 380). These fair use principles, which are found in section 107 of the Copyright Act (1976) are explained below.

FAIR USE FACTOR 1: PURPOSE AND CHARACTER OF USE

The first fair use factor, purpose and character of use, looks at how the person copying the work is going to use it. Works copied for educational, nonprofit, or personal purposes are much more likely to be considered within fair use than are those items that are copied for the purposes of earning money. Thus, a teacher may be able to copy an article on prairie dogs for a class of 27 students studying the fauna of the western United States, but not for the purpose of selling the article. A good question for you to ask yourself here is, "What do I want to do with the materials I plan to copy?"[1]

FAIR USE FACTOR 2: NATURE OF THE WORK

The second fair use factor, the nature of the work, deals with the work's characteristics: is the work fact or fiction, published or unpublished? Works most usable under fair use factor #2 are nonfiction published pieces. This means that a travel magazine article about the Yanomamo Indians of Venezuela and Brazil might be copy-able for a social studies class, while an unpublished PowerPoint or fictionalized story about the same Indians might not be. Good questions for you to ask yourself here are, "Is this work fact or fiction? Has this work been published or not?"

FAIR USE FACTOR 3: QUANTITY TO BE BORROWED

The third fair use factor covers the quantity of work one plans to borrow. For example, do you want to use an entire hour-long video tape or just five minutes of it? Are you interested in copying the Beatles' song "Hard Day's Night" in its entirety or just a small part of it? With this fair use factor, the smallest amount borrowed is usually the best. This factor is measured two ways: quantitatively and qualitatively. "Quantity considers the amount copied relative to the whole original as well as the amount needed to achieve the objective of the copying. Qualitative measurement is more creative. It involves the concept of substantiality, whereby copying the "heart" of the work—no matter how small—is too much" (Butler, 2001a, 35). Thus, five minutes of an hour-long video recording about what seals eat would fit into this guideline—unless that particular five minutes was the *heart* of the recording; i.e., showing what the seal actually eats. Good questions for you to ask yourself here are, "How much do I need to borrow? Is this the heart of the work?"

FAIR USE FACTOR 4: MARKETABILITY OF THE WORK

The fourth fair use factor features the marketability of the work. In essence, this means that if this work were to be copied and sold, either as part of a newly created item or by itself, would such a sale affect the amount of money that the owner or creator of the work could earn from it? For instance, if copying an extra script of a high school play means that the publisher who owns the rights to that play does not get royalties, then such copying is in violation of the law. Another example is that dealing with sheet music. Here we will use a band director as the case in point. Perhaps the director finds that there is one student too many in the clarinet section. That student needs a copy of the second clarinet part for the concert coming up in three weeks. The band director de-cides to make one copy—after all, the music selection was purchased for the whole band! Unfortunately, unless there is no other way to get the clarinet part before the concert, such copying may be in violation. In addition, if the concert is imminent and a copy is made, that copy needs to be destroyed right after the concert, unless the copyright holder granted proper permission. A good question to ask yourself here is, "Will my copying this item mean that the copyright holder will earn less money?"[2]

COPYRIGHT GUIDELINES FOR EDUCATIONAL MULTIMEDIA

The four "fair use factors" discussed above are very important to K-12 teachers as they work with new and old technologies, with students and colleagues. However, these four factors were purposefully written so they are vague (Rose, 1993) in order to permit flexibility in their use—which makes many teachers uncomfortable when they are trying to use all or part of a copyrighted work. Thus, teachers may want to have an exact amount in mind when considering how much they can and can't copy without permission. This is where the Fair Use Guidelines for Educa-tional Multimedia (Consortium of College and University Multimedia Centers [CCUMC], 2002) come into play.

These guidelines are more rigid than the four fair use factors discussed above (Crews, 2001). Because of this, most copyright experts do not en-courage their use. They are covered here because, while they do not have the power of law, ". . . they give the courts a sense of how lawmakers intend fair use to be interpreted . . ." (Butler, 2001b: 34). Originally de-veloped by the CCUMC (2002), when this organization participated in the Conference on Fair Use,[3] these guidelines are *solely* applied to the creation and use of educational multimedia and represent the minimum, rather than the maximum, of what is represented by fair use. Therefore, when creating a multimedia presentation for a class with excerpts from a video, CD, audio-tape, televised cartoon, book, etc., the numbers in Figure 2-1 can be applied.

Two copies (one for viewing and one for reserve) in addition to one for each of the creators of the multimedia presentation may be made and kept. While these copies can be kept and used for two years, after that time period, if you want to keep using the project, then you will need to obtain permissions. These permissions will have to be obtained from everyone from whom you borrowed, whether the borrowing origi-nally fit under the fair use guidelines or not. However, the multimedia

Figure 2–1
Quantities of Media Recommended for Borrowing under
the Fair Use Guidelines for Educational Multimedia

Medium	Amount
Motion Media	10% or three minutes
Text	10% or 1,000 words
Poems of Less Than 250 Words	three poems
Poems over 250 Words	up to 250 words
	three excerpts by a poet
	five excerpts by different poets in same collection
Music, Lyrics, Music Video	up to 10% or 30 seconds
Illustrations and Photographs	five by the same artist or photographer
	10% or 15 images from one published work
Numerical Data Sets	10% or 2,500 fields or cells (Penn State Libraries, 1997)

Remember, when borrowing without permission from copyrighted works, use the smallest quantity that you can.

project can be kept intact after the two years, without obtaining permissions, if used by the creator(s) for a portfolio, (unpaid) workshop, or presentation for peers (Penn State Libraries, 1997; Lehman, 1996).

CONCLUSION

As has been stated earlier in this chapter, copyright is a very gray issue. This also means that those interpreting the four fair use factors may not always agree on interpretations. Because such lack of agreement is often the case, it is important to remember that all four of the fair use factors need to be followed in order for any copying to be considered legal (Besenjak, 1997; Bruwelheide, 1995).[4]

END NOTES

1. The making of parodies and other transformations of works also come under the first fair use factor. Such use is allowed "for purposes such as criticism [or] comment . . ." (U.S. Copyright Law, 1976, Section 107, 16). For more information on this, see chapter 10: "Music/Audio and Copyright Law."

2. Since the mid-1990s, the licensing of works is now also being considered in evaluating this factor with "for-profit organizations." This is a result of *American Geophysical Union et al. v. Texaco Inc.* (1992) in which several Texaco scientists were found to have violated copyright law by copying a number of scientific journal articles without paying royalties to the publishers. Part of the out-of-court settlement involved paying a licensing fee retroactively to the Copyright Clearance Center. This case does not apply to nonprofit educational institutions or library copying as covered in Section 108 of the 1976 Copyright Act (Wiant, 1998).

3. The Conference on Fair Use (CONFU) first convened in 1994. It was composed of a number of individuals representing such user organizations as the American Library Association and the National Education Association and such owner groups as the Motion Picture Association of America and the Software Publishers Association. The purpose of CONFU was to discuss fair use and develop guidelines for librarians and educators to use when working with copyrighted works. The CONFU concept was that such guidelines would be agreeable to both users and owners (Lehman, 1996, 2). Overall, representatives of the two groups found it difficult to agree on copyright guidelines: user groups tended to feel that the suggested guidelines were too stringent; owner groups felt that the same guidelines were not strong enough (Butler, 2002).

4. There are exceptions to almost every rule, and the fair use factors are not exempt. For example, copying, in excess of the four fair use factors, is allowed at times for disabled users, depending on the disability, and how the copying is made and used. Such exemptions are addressed in more depth in later chapters.

REFERENCES

American Geophysical Union et al. v. Texaco Inc. 1992. 802 F. (S.D.N.Y.).

Besenjak, Cheryl. 1997. *Copyright Plain & Simple.* Franklin Lakes, NJ: Career Press.

Bruwelheide, Janis H. 1995. *The Copyright Primer for Librarians and Educators.* 2nd ed. Chicago: American Library Association.

Butler, Rebecca P. 2001a. "Copyright as a Social Responsibility—Fair Use: I Need It Now!" *Knowledge Quest* 29, no. 3 (January/February): 35–36.

———. 2001b. "Fair Use Guidelines for Educational Multimedia." *Knowledge Quest* 29, no. 4 (March/April): 34–35.

Consortium of College and University Centers (CCUMC), Ames, IA.

2002. CCUMC Copyright Initiatives (August). Available: www.ccumc.org/copyright/initiatives.html (accessed June 7, 2004).

Crews, Kenneth D. 2001. "Faculty and Student Issues" Panel presentation at Northern Illinois University Conference on Copyright and Intellectual Property Issues for Online Instruction, DeKalb, IL, September 28.

Lawrence, John S., and Bernard Timberg. 1989. *Fair Use and Free Inquiry: Copyright Law and the New Media.* 2nd ed. Norwood, NJ: Ablex.

Lehman, Bruce A. 1996. *The Conference on Fair Use: An Interim Report to the Commissioner.* Washington, DC: U.S. Patent and Trademark Office.

Penn State Libraries: AV Services. 1997. "Highlights of the Fair Use Guidelines for Educational Multimedia." (April). Available: www.libraries.psu.edu/mtss/fairuse/fairuseguide.ppt (accessed June 7, 2004).

Rose, Mark. 1993. *Authors and Owners: The Invention of Copyright.* Cambridge, MA: Harvard University Press.

U.S. Copyright Law. 1976. Public Law 94-553, sec. 107, 16.

Wiant, Sarah K. 1998. "Appendix 1: *American Geophysical Union, et al. v. Texaco Inc.*" Washington, DC: Association of Research Libraries. (March). Available: www.arl.org/scomm/cppsc/wiant.html (accessed June 7, 2004).

Chapter Three

Public Domain: Is There Such a Thing as Free Material?

INTRODUCTION

Working in the K-12 school environment, educators use a number of reasons for borrowing material without permission. Such reasons include (1) This is a nonprofit educational institution, so it's OK. (2) No one will know anyway. (3) It's for the kids, they need it, and we can't afford to purchase it. As will be seen throughout this book, such arguments are often in direct contrast to copyright law. However at times, there actually *may* be free material that you can use. Such material is in the public domain.

WHAT IS PUBLIC DOMAIN?

Essentially, works in the public domain are free to use any way that you want. For example, Grimm's fairy tales, including "Cinderella" and "Snow White," are in the public domain. This means that you can change these stories into new ones, based on modern times, for your class; print out the new stories for all students in your school; even sell copies of these stories at a school fair. Thus, public domain also encourages creation of new works. What is not in the public domain is a revised fairy tale (one that someone else has already changed). Thus, while "Cinderella" is in the public domain, the Disney version of it (whether book or movie) is not.[1]

When using public domain materials, you can borrow all or part of a work—print or nonprint, fiction or nonfiction—and not worry about copyright infringement. The idea behind public domain is that the copyright owner has given up, to the public at large, all of his or her original rights to the work (see chapter 1 for the list of original rights).

HOW LONG DOES IT TAKE A WORK TO BECOME PART OF PUBLIC DOMAIN?

Public domain used to follow copyright law as it existed at the time of the creation or publication of the work. The Copyright Term Extension Act (CTEA) was passed in October 1998, and there are now exceptions to this rule. CTEA changes U.S. copyright law by extending the term of copyright protection for works created January 1, 1978, or after from the life of the author plus 50 years to the international criterion of life plus 70 years (and works for hire to 95 years from publication or 120 years after creation) (Hoffmann, 2001; Torrans, 2003).[2] This is very confusing, and is a result of U.S. Copyright Law being amended many times since its inception. Because of this, "No simple statement can be made to the effect that 'the term of protection for Y types of works is X years.' Rather, works of the same type but produced at different times will often have different terms of protection . . ." (Karjala, 2002, 1). Still, some rules apply:

1. Works published before 1923 are in the public domain.
2. Works published between 1923 and 1963, when a copyright notice is attached, can have their copyright renewed for a total of 67 years beyond the date of publication. (However, if the copyright is not renewed[3] or if the work originally had no official copyright notice,[4] then the work is already in public domain.)
3. For works published from 1964 to 1977 with an official copyright notice attached, copyright is automatically renewed for a total of 95 years.
4. Works created but not published before January 1, 1978,[5] are legally copyrighted for the life of the owner plus 70 years.
5. All works published on or after January 1, 1978, are copyrighted for the lifetime of the creator/owner plus 70 years (Butler, 2001, 47–48; Karjala, 2002). (If there is more than one creator/owner, the 70-year rule applies based on the lifetime of the longest living copyright holder.) If works have a corporate author or are "work for hire,"[6] then works published on or after January 1, 1978, are copyrighted for 120 years after the date of creation or 95 years from publication, the lesser amount being the one that applies (Torrans, 2003). This is a direct result of the Sonny Bono Copyright Term Extension Act of 1998 (Public Law Number 105–298) mentioned

above in this chapter.[7] Because the Sonny Bono Act is retroactive, this means that the earliest any work copyrighted after 1978 can come into the public domain is January 1, 2048.

Are There Any Simple Strategies for Knowing What Is Definitely in Public Domain at the Present?

While the terms simple strategies and public domain appear to be polar opposites, below are a few guidelines that apply. Works definitely in the public domain include those:

1. published before 1923,
2. published between 1923 and 1963 with a copyright notice but no renewal of copyright,
3. published between 1923 and 1978 with no copyright notice,
4. published between 1978 and March 1, 1989, with no copyright notice and no registration (Butler, 2001; Gasaway, 2001),
5. to which the author/owner has given up all rights.

IF THERE IS NO COPYRIGHT DATE ON A WORK DOES THAT MEAN IT IS IN THE PUBLIC DOMAIN?

Do not assume, that because no copyright date can be found on a work, it is automatically in the public domain. "Since March 1, 1989, the inclusion of a copyright notice on any form of material has been optional, but recommended . . ." (Bruwelheide, 1995, 60). This includes all kinds of works: books, newspaper articles, music CDs, DVDs or videos, computer software, or the Internet. It is good to remember that most works in the public domain are there because their copyright term has expired.

WHAT IF THE WORK IS CREATED AS PART OF THE TERMS OF EMPLOYMENT?

If a work is created as part of an employee's job description or is work "for hire," then the organization that employs the creator owns the copyright for either the publication date plus 95 years or 120 years from the time of creation—the shorter term applying. After that, the work will be in public domain. For example, this means that if you created a Web page for your school's library media center using school time, computers, and software that the school would own your work for 95–120 years.[8] For those things published between 1923 and 1978, the term of copyright varies, based on what the copyright law stated at the time of publication (Gasaway, 2001). A general rule is to assume that whatever you want to use is still under copyright, unless there is a statement on or near the item, clearly indicating that it is in public domain. This includes the Internet.[9]

WHAT WORKS ARE IN THE PUBLIC DOMAIN?

Works in the public domain include:
- most federal documents,[10]
- phone books,
- works with expired copyrights,
- works for which creators/owners have chosen to give up their copyrights,
- freeware,[11]
- things that cannot be copyrighted, for example, names, short phrases, titles, ideas, and facts,
- some clip art (Internet and print),
- works published in 1923 or before, and
- some works published between 1923 and 1963 (Bruwelheide, 1995; Butler 2001; Gasaway, 2001).

Do You Have to Purchase Public Domain Material or Is It Free?[12]

Public domain materials, just like other works, may be free, as in the cases of an Internet site that states it is in the public domain or free software found on the Web.[13] Public domain materials may also be sold, although the cost is usually not as much as works that carry copyright notices. For example, someone could take the U.S. Constitution, Bill of Rights, and Declaration of Independence and print them up in booklet form for purchase. While these three pieces of United States history are in the public domain, a printed booklet containing them might be sold for replication costs and whatever the printer thinks could be earned over and above that. No royalty expenses need be figured into the cost. Public domain "offers cheap content—to be used, reformulated, and recast." (Public Knowledge, n.d., 1).[14]

ARE ALL FEDERAL GOVERNMENT DOCUMENTS IN THE PUBLIC DOMAIN?

Federal government documents, created as work for hire, are not copyrighted. As such, they are in the public domain. Examples of such documents are House and Senate legislation, texts of federal court decisions, agency circulars, and federal reports. However, if the federal government hires outside contractors to produce works, such works may or may not be copyrighted—depending on the contract between the government and the contracted individuals or company. Say, for example, that the federal government hires a historian to write a definitive history of the House of Representatives. If the contract between the government and the historian says that copyright ownership is the historian's, or does not state who will own the copyright, then ownership stays with the historian. If this contract states, instead, that the work is for hire, then the government owns the copyright. In addition, the federal government can own the copyrights to works transferred to it. This means, if you transfer the copyright to an educational Web site on Alaskan king crabs—one you created as a classroom unit—to the Department of Education (DOE), then the DOE will own whatever copyrights came with your gift.[15] There is a third instance in which federal government documents are *not* public domain material. This is when an individual or organization takes a federal government document in the public domain and adds original elements, such as critiques, indexing criteria, conclusions, summaries, or other original elements to it. In such a case, the individual or group creating the document derivative can claim copyright to the derivative parts. Thus, there is no specific rule to federal government documents and public domain (Bruwelheide, 1995; Copyright Website, 2002; Crews, 2000).[16] If in doubt, ". . . examine each item closely, and inquire with the author or the issuing agency" (Crews, 2000, 16).

ARE STATE AND LOCAL GOVERNMENT DOCUMENTS IN THE PUBLIC DOMAIN?

The answer to this question depends on the state or local government. For the purposes of copyright law,[17] these agencies—considered owners of works in much the same way as individuals or companies—may choose the works for which they want to own the copyright and the works they want to place in the public domain.[18] Again, there is no one rule, guideline, or principle. Therefore, it is best to check with a particular state or local government agency for information on public domain materials (Bruwelheide, 1995; Crews, 2000). The information you need may be accessible from:

1. a state office—for instance, an individual in the Legislative Information System in Springfield, Illinois (Leah Sia, personal communication, Oct. 13, 2003),
2. the State Attorney's Office in your county seat, and/or

3. the city manager's secretary (Leah Sia, personal communication, Nov. 25, 2003).

Information may be just an e-mail or phone call away.

IS SOMETHING THAT IS IN THE PUBLIC DOMAIN IN ANOTHER COUNTRY ALSO IN THE PUBLIC DOMAIN IN THE UNITED STATES?

The United States is a member of a number of international treaties that cover or are concerned with copyright law. Generally, when a work is disseminated in the United States, U.S. law applies, and when an item is distributed overseas, the laws of the particular countries receiving the item apply. For example, *Peter Pan* is copyrighted in the United Kingdom, but is in the public domain in the United States (Project Gutenberg, 2002). However, there are exceptions to this rule as is discussed below.

CAN SOMETHING BE TAKEN OUT OF THE PUBLIC DOMAIN AND PLACED UNDER COPYRIGHT PROTECTION AGAIN?

Copyright law, as written by our forebearers and current lawmakers, is a very gray issue. Public domain is no exception. For example, the Uruguay Round Agreements Act of 1994 implements the General Agreement on Tariffs and Trade (GATT Treaty). One result of the GATT is that as of January 1, 1996, a number of foreign works, at that time in the public domain in the United States, were placed back under copyright protection.[19] This was because they were still under copyright in their own countries (Besenjak, 1997; Sinofsky, 2000). What this means for us as educators, is that how much of an artwork we can copy, put on a Web site, blow up for a bulletin board, for our class multimedia art project may depend on whether we are using a U.S. or German edition of the work. For more information on international copyright protection, see chapter 5.

HOW DO YOU KNOW THAT AN ITEM IS IN THE PUBLIC DOMAIN?

The best answer is to find out when the item was first copyrighted[20] and then figure it out based on copyright law. An easier approach is to look for a statement on the item in question. If it says that it is public domain material, it probably is.[21] For example, a clip-art Web-site owner may have a statement at the beginning or end of his or her Web page stating that it is in the public domain. This means that you should be able to borrow any of the clip art from this site and use it in any manner that you wish. Do be aware, however, that a site owner or administrator could feasibly take art from a copyrighted site and put it on his or her site without your knowledge. Thus, you could, in good faith, borrow a piece of copyrighted art from a site that supposedly was in the public domain. The best advice in cases like this is to make sure that clip art you use is from a reputable site. For instance, a reputable clip-art site might be one obtained from a prominent software company's Web page.

How Do You Make Sure That What You Are Borrowing Is Really in the Public Domain?

Since users or borrowers of works must often rely on media documentation that an item is in public domain, the best solution is to choose public domain material from reputable sites (Internet); publishing companies (books, articles, recordings, software, etc.); or vendors.

While public domain material cannot be "re-copyrighted," except foreign works, it is possible to alter a public domain piece and create a derivative work. When this happens, as was discussed above in this chapter, the pieces of the public domain work that were changed can be placed back under copyright protection. A work by Shakespeare can serve as an example. Shakespeare's works are in the public domain. However, an artist may illustrate a copy of *Hamlet* by sketching scenes from the play in the margins or drawing beautiful curlicue letters to begin each act. If this artist wishes, she or he can then sell this newly illustrated copy of *Hamlet*, copy it, or display it in public. In other words, since original work has been added to alter *Hamlet*, the artist now owns this particular version of the play and the copyright to it.

CONCLUSION

Is public domain a good thing? Teachers and librarians often find themselves wanting more for less. Here public domain materials may help, for with them you may copy, create derivatives, and, in essence, use such materials any way you want as you strive to teach your students and better support your curriculums.

Just remember—if a work does not state it is in the public domain, assume it has a copyright, unless it was published before 1923.

END NOTES

1. The Disney version is not in the public domain, because the revised portion(s) of this work, derivatives of the original piece, are protected under copyright law. Thus, while the story of "Cinderella" remains in the public domain, a cartoon version, or any other revision of the story, may be copyrighted.
2. CTEA applies retrospectively as well as prospectively to all works still under copyright on the bill's effective date, October 27, 1998.
3. A question that arises here is, how would one know if a copyright had been renewed or not? If renewed, the new copyright date would be listed on the verso page of a newer version of a book or in the area where copyright information is listed for other works. However, this would not answer the question for older works, which would only contain the original copyright date. For such older works, it is possible to obtain public domain information by contacting the U.S. Copyright Office. While the Copyright Office does not compile or maintain lists of public domain materials, it can conduct a search to find the answer (for a fee), or you may search their records online yourself (without the fee) (U.S. Copyright Office, 1999).
4. Authors and owners of works are not required to put a copyright notice on their creations (Bruwelheide, 1995).
5. January 1, 1978, is the effective date of the 1976 Copyright Act (Butler, 2001).
6. Work for hire occurs when a company or individual commissions another to create a work and a contract to that effect is signed before the work begins (Besenjak, 1997, 30).
7. The reasoning behind this act was to bring the U.S. copyright term of ownership under the same conditions as that of many European nations, thus giving U.S. owners of works the same protection as that afforded European owners (Sinofsky, 2000).
8. Because the Internet is so new, the only way a Web site can be in the public domain is if the author/owner of the work chooses to place it there.
9. It is a misconception that the Internet, because it is so accessible, is free, i.e., not copyrighted (Simpson, 2001).
10. See the section in this chapter entitled, "Are All Federal Government Documents in the Public Domain?" for discussion on which federal documents are in the public domain and which are not.
11. Freeware is unlicensed software. It can be loaned and used without restraint (Bruwelheide, 1995).

12. Because educators are often on tight budgets and looking to cut costs, this question can be important to the classroom teacher and other school faculty and staff.
13. An example of a site that promotes free software is www.gnu.org/.
14. It is possible to copyright re-printed public domain materials if there are any changes to the works, for example, if the materials were not originally packaged together, there is a new collection title, there is a graphic added to the collection that was not available with the originals, etc. (Again, be aware that in reality, only the revised sections of the public domain work are being copyrighted; that which remains original is still in the public domain.)
15. Remember: you should always try to transfer copyrights via written documents.
16. According to "Wikipedia: Public Domain Resources," ". . . material that is generated by the Federal government which doesn't have a notice can be copied" (Wikipedia, 2004, 1). (Author note: It is possible that there are exceptions to this comment; therefore, if you are unsure, I encourage you to contact the document author or issuing agency or department.)
17. Copyright law is federal legislation (Cornell University, 2003).
18. State and local government documents include state legislative materials, texts of state and local court cases, minutes of city council meetings, birth and death records, tax files, real estate transactions, county board proceedings, etc.
19. These works were from a number of countries, including Japan, Germany, and several Spanish-speaking countries. Titles varied from *Hipokuratesu-tachi* to *Echo der Heimat* to *Aguiluchos Mexicanos* (*Federal Register*, 1998).
20. The easiest way to determine the first copyright date is to look for the oldest of the copyright dates listed on the work in question. Also, remember: copyright can be registered from either the date of publication or the date of creation.
21. Probably is an operative word here, since hypothetically it is possible to label a work in the public domain when it is still under copyright.

REFERENCES

Besenjak, Cheryl. 1997. *Copyright Plain & Simple*. Franklin Lakes, NJ: Career Press.

Bruwelheide, Janis H. 1995. *The Copyright Primer for Librarians and Educators*, 2nd ed. Chicago: American Library Association.

Butler, Rebecca P. 2001. "Public Domain: What It Is and How It Works." *Knowledge Quest* 29, no. 5 (May/June): 47–48.

——. 2002. "Software Piracy: Don't Let It Byte You!" *Knowledge Quest* 31, no. 2 (November/December): 41–42.

Copyright Website. 2002. "Copyright Basics: Public Domain." Foster City, CA: Copyright Website LLC. Available: www.benedict.com/info/publicDomain/publicDomain.asp (accessed June 7, 2004).

Cornell University, Legal Information Institute. 2003. "Copyright: An Overview." Ithaca, NY: Cornell University. (November) Available: www.law.cornell.edu/topics/copyright.html (accessed June 2, 2004).

Crews, Kenneth D. 2000. *Copyright Essentials for Librarians and Educators.* Chicago: American Library Association.

Federal Register. 1998. Vol. 63, no. 157 (August 14): Docket No. 97-3E. Available as "Federal Register Notice" at www.copyright.gov/fedreg/1998/63fr43830.html (accessed June 7, 2004).

Free Software Foundation. 2003. "GNU's Not Unix!—The GNU Project and the Free Software Foundation (FSF)." Boston: Free Software Foundation. (October). Available: www.gnu.org/ (accessed June 2, 2004).

Gasaway, Lolly. 2001. "When Works Pass into the Public Domain." Chapel Hill: The University of North Carolina. (September). Available: www.unc.edu/~unclung/public-d.htm (accessed June 2, 2004).

Hoffmann, Gretchen McCord. 2001. *Copyright in Cyberspace: Questions and Answers for Librarians.* New York: Neal-Schuman.

Karjala, Dennis S. 2002. "Chart Showing Changes Made and the Degree of Harmonization Achieved and Disharmonization Exacerbated by the Sonny Bono Copyright Term Extension Act (CETA)." Tempe: AZ State University. (May). Available: http://homepages.law.asu.edu/%7Edkarjala/OpposingCopyrightExtension/legmats/HarmonizationChartDSK.html (accessed June 7, 2004).

Project Gutenberg Official Home Site. 2002. "Public Domain and Copyright How-To." Oxford, MS: Project Gutenberg Literary Archive Foundation. (June). Available: http://promo.net/pg/vol/pd.html (accessed June 6, 2004).

Public Knowledge. N.D. "Why Public Domain Matters." Washington, DC: Public Knowledge. Available: www.publicknowledge.org/public_domain/public_domain_intro/view?searchterm=the%20economic%20value%20of%20the%20public%20domain (accessed June 7, 2004).

Simpson, Carol. 2001. *Copyright for Schools: A Practical Guide.* 3rd ed. Worthington, OH: Linworth.

Sinofsky, Esther R. 2000. "The Privatization of Public Domain?" *TechTrends* 44, no. 2 (March): 11–13.

Torrans, Lee Ann. 2003. *Law for K-12 Libraries and Librarians.* Westport, CT: Libraries Unlimited.

U.S. Copyright Office, Library of Congress. 1999. "Frequently Asked Questions." Available: lcweb.loc.gov/copyright/faq.html (accessed June 2, 2004).

Wikipedia, The Free Encyclopedia. 2004. "Wikipedia: Public Domain Resources." Available: http://en.wikipedia.org/wiki/Wikipedia:Public_domain_resources#US_Government (accessed June 2, 2004).

Chapter Four

Obtaining Permission: How Can You Legally Obtain Use of Works?

As a teacher or librarian you are often concerned with how you can make sure that you are not violating copyright when you use or copy a work. This chapter will look at how to obtain permission from the author or owner of a work—the ideal way of making sure that you are following the law.

Let's imagine that you, as the physical education teacher, have a specific video (a popular entertainment video that you purchased at a local store) that you would like to show to all classes in the school the afternoon before winter vacation. This is to be the students' reward for a semester of hard work on a "Junior Olympics" project. The principal has agreed to assemble the students in the auditorium for the showing of this video if you are able to obtain permission to use it in such a manner. The first thing you do is go to your school media specialist, who tells you, since the video is for entertainment rather than an instructional purpose,[2] that you need to obtain the right to perform it in public before it can be shown in the auditorium. You are pretty sure that you did not purchase such rights when you bought it. Therefore, with the help of your school library media specialist, you will have to identify and find the owner or creator of the video and obtain permission from this person(s). Let's look first at what permission is all about.

OBTAINING PERMISSION

Sometimes, the owner of a work will state up front in the work that permission is being given to a user for certain rights. One example of this is from a Web page created by Brad Templeton: "Permission is granted to freely print, unmodified, up to 100 copies of the most up-to-date version of this document from <www.templetons.com/brad/copymyths.html>, or to copy it in off-the-net electronic form" (Templeton, 1995). If that is the case, then the would-be user simply follows the copyright owner's specifications. But what happens when the owner has not placed any usage agreements, other than a copyright notice, on the product? Well, you ask for the rights that you need from the owner or purchase a license to use or copy the work. (How to find copyright owners and clearinghouses for copyrighted works will be addressed later in this chapter.) Remember that the copyright owner has the right to either give, sell, or refuse your request to use the work.

Permission Requests

It is always best to put requests in writing so that you have a record of the permission criteria, should any disagreements occur between you and the copyright owner or clearinghouse. If that is not possible, then take notes of your oral conversation with the copyright owner or clearinghouse and keep them on file for future reference. Once you have found the owner of the work, information that should be included in the permission request is as follows:

1. Identify what it is that you want permission to use by author, title, format, and other identifiers.
2. Determine what kind of permission you need; that is, how, where, how many times, and how long are you going to use this item? (For example, given your video question, you need permission to show the video one time, in an auditorium, for the entire school population.)

Remember to request permission as early as possible. There is no time limit to replies, and just because you do not hear from an owner, it does not mean that she or he has tacitly agreed that you may use the work(s). Thus, you may find that you need to follow up on permission requests, or contact another source if you find out that the organization you contact it is not the owner. Also, if the request is answered in the negative, starting early gives you time to find something you can substitute (Fulcrum, n.d.).

WHAT IS A LICENSE?

A license lends the user the rights of the work that have been obtained from the owner, or an organization representing the owner. For example, the American Society of Composers, Authors and Publishers (ASCAP, 2003), which functions as a clearinghouse representing a large number of those who compose, write, and publish music, assigns those who obtain one of their licenses, the "right to perform ANY or ALL of the musical works in our repertory" (Innes, 2000). One such group that might help you resolve your video use question (above) would be the Motion Picture Licensing Corp. <www.mplc.com>, which "Licenses 'public performances' of pre-existing video, for example a movie you've rented from the local Blockbuster, or a clip from an industry video" (ASCAP, 2004).

GIVE CREDIT WHERE CREDIT IS DUE

Payment is not necessarily required for permission. The owner or author may want nothing more than to be recognized for his or her work. Thus, always give credit to copyright owner(s) in a reference or citation section at either the beginning or end of the use or presentation of the work and follow any stipulations for the format of the citation.[3] However, while technically payment is not required for permission, it is possible that the work's owner(s) will request that you pay a fee or purchase a license before you are allowed to use the work.

PERMISSION LETTER

For the purposes of this exercise, assume you are requesting clearance to use a video for a public showing. Formats other than videos may require different criteria and will be discussed below. (Criteria need to match the format and type of request that you are using or need.) Sample general information includes the following:

- author, title, format;
- type of permission you are asking for (how often you will use the work, length of time of use, number of copies needed, intended audience, and whether or not you will be charging your audience for use of the work);
- your name, address, phone and fax numbers, e-mail;
- your signature; and
- a place for the copyright holder's signature.

The following information should be included in a letter requesting appropriate permission.

Print

- volume number
- edition
- ISBN (book) or ISSN (magazine) number
- editor, compiler, or translater
- publisher
- place of publication
- copyright date
- page, figure, table, or illustration identifiers
- a copy of what you want to borrow

Nonprint

- how the borrowed item (multimedia project, online class, etc.) will be used
- distributor
- where you plan to use or market your creation
- expected date of publication or use (if appropriate)
- copyright date
- URL, site manager, name of site (if part or all of a Web site)
- footage amount (if a video or television program)

You may also add a date by which you would like to hear back from the copyright owners. While they do not need to comply with your request, it may be an incentive to their granting permission information more quickly. In addition, you may wish to ask them to provide you with the correct copyright owner, if you have sent your permission request to the wrong place. It is also important to thank those from whom you are requesting permission for their time and effort in providing you the use of their copyrighted item(s).

Remember, the more complete the information that you include in your request, the quicker the response time may be (Bellingham Public Schools, 2003; Illinois Association of School Boards, 1999; Harper, 2001a; Talub, 2001).

Send the request-for-permission letter to the copyright owner, clearance center, distributor or publisher of the work(s).

Sending and Receiving the Permission Letter

Including a stamped, self-addressed envelope (SASE) may speed up response time.

Figure 4–1
Sample Request for Permission

Your name and address (letterhead)

Date

Name and address of copyright owner or publisher

Dear _____,

    I would like to request permission to show the video [citation: including such things as title, copyright date, distributor, publisher] to the students of _____High School on [date] in the high school auditorium. This will be a one-time showing. The purpose of this showing is to reward the students of my school for their participation in our Junior Olympics program.

    Could you please sign this letter below, if willing to grant permission, and return to me by [date] or as soon as possible? Also, if I should be contacting someone other than you for this request, could you provide me with the name and address of the party to contact?

    I have included an SASE for your use. Thank you for considering my request.

Sincerely,
(Your name)

    PERMISSION GIVEN FOR _____ TO USE MY VIDEO, [title], ON [date specified above].

DATE:

SIGNATURE:

(Bellingham Public School, 2003; Illinois Association of School Boards, 1999; Harper, 2001; Talub, 2001)

Make sure that the permission is both sent and received either in a letter, fax, or e-mail form. It is imperative that you have a written record of all copyright permissions granted. This way no one can come back at a later date and say, "I did not say that," or "That's not what I meant."

Figure 4–1 is an example of a letter that you might use for the video question from above.

CLEARINGHOUSES AND OTHER ORGANIZATIONS

If you are unable to find the owners or authors of a work, where do you send your request for permission to use or copy their work(s)? Well, you can go to the publisher of the work for contact information. You can also go to an organization, such as an agency or royalty house, company, or clearinghouse that specializes in helping users obtain copyright clearance. Such a group, usually for a fee,[4] will work with you to obtain the proper clearance or license that is needed. Thus, the type of work that you need permission to use or copy determines where you go to find permission or further information. Below, are some of the places that you may go online to obtain permissions. In most cases, these groups charge a fee.

Cartoons

United Media: <www.unitedmedia.com> For those users who want to place a cartoon on a Web page, in a multimedia production, on an overhead, etc., United Media can provide permission and fee information.

Universal Press Syndicate: <www.uexpress.com> This organization operates the same way as United Media.

Images

Kodak: <http://kodak.com/UK/en/corp/permission.shtml> This area of the Eastman Kodak Company works with users who request permission to copy Kodak material for other than private/noncommercial use.

Media Image Resource Alliance (MIRA): <www.mira.com> MIRA is an agency within the Copyright Clearance Center (see below under "Other"). Through MIRA, users may view images online and obtain permission to use/publish them.

Music[5]

American Society of Composers, Authors and Publishers (ASCAP): <www.ascap.com> "ASCAP licenses the right to perform songs and musical works created and owned by songwriters, composers, lyricists and music publishers who are ASCAP members and members of foreign performing rights organizations who are represented by ASCAP in the United States" (American Society of Composers, Authors and Publishers, 2003).

Broadcast Music, Inc. (BMI): <http://bmi.com/home.asp> BMI represents over 300,000 songwriters, composers, and music publishers and over 4.5 million works in all styles of music. The purchase of a BMI license enables a user to play musical works by anyone whom the organization represents (Broadcast Music, Inc., 2003).

Harry Fox Agency: <www.nmpa.org/hfa.html> One of the features of this agency is that it licenses mechanical rights so that the user may use sound recordings in conjunction with multimedia productions, including such things as PowerPoint.

Recording Industry Association of America (RIAA): <www.riaa.com> This organization, which represents many major recording labels, assists users in obtaining permission to use copyrighted recordings.

SESAC, Inc.: <www.sesac.com/non_flash_home.htm> "Performing rights organizations, such as SESAC, are businesses designed to represent songwriters and publishers and their right to be compensated for having their music performed in public. By securing a license from SESAC, for example, music users (i.e., television and radio stations, auditoriums, restaurants, hotels, theme parks, malls, funeral homes, etc.) can legally play any song in the SESAC repertory. Without a license from a performing rights organization, music users are in danger of copyright infringement" (SESAC, 2003).

Print

UnCover: <www.ingenta.com> UnCover is a "collective-licensing agency representing such writers' groups as The National Writers Union (NWU), the Canadian Science Writers' Association (CSWA) . . . the Society of Children's Book Writers and Illustrators . . ." and others (Harper, 2001a).

Religious

Christian Copyright Licensing International (CCLI): <www.ccli.com> For an annual fee, this organization will provide religious groups with a license that covers the use of over 150,000 pieces of religious music.

Theatrical Performances

Musical Theatrical International (MTI): <www.mtishows.com/licensing.htm> MTI offers online applications to obtain licenses for many musicals (both professional and amateur performances).

Video and Motion Pictures

Motion Picture Licensing Corporation: <www.mplc.com/index2.htm> "The Motion Picture Licensing Corporation (MPLC) is an independent copyright licensing service exclusively authorized by major Hollywood motion picture studios and independent producers to grant Umbrella Licenses to non-profit groups, businesses and government organizations for the public performances of home videocassettes and videodiscs" (Motion Picture Licensing Corporation, 2003).

Other

Copyright Clearance Center (CCC): <www.copyright.com> This clearinghouse provides licensing agreements for a wide variety of both print and electronic works. The CCC can also help users locate hard-to-find or unregistered copyright holders. One of the features of the CCC is their "Republication Licensing Service," which presents the user with the option of requesting and receiving permission and paying royalty fees to "republish excerpts of copyrighted works—in print, electronically, or both!" ("Zip through Permissions," 2003).

U.S. Copyright Office: <www.loc.gov/copyright/circs/circ22.html#searching> For a fee ($65.00/hour), the U.S. Copyright Office will search its records to find permission information.

Obtaining copyright permission for any work can be challenging. Remember—when requesting permission for a work, obtain your license or user/borrower agreement in writing, and be sure to follow all stipulations of the agreement. And keep in mind, you can always ask your school media specialist for help.

END NOTES

1. Please note: Chapter Four is largely based on three articles first published as Butler, Rebecca P. 2001. "Obtaining Permission to Copy or Perform a Work," Parts I–III. *Knowledge Quest* 30, no. 2 (November/December): 43–44; no. 3 (January/February): 32–33; and no. 4 (March/April): 45–46.
2. Video owners' copyrights are limited in that videos used for instructional purposes in nonprofit educational institutions can be displayed without infringement (U.S. Copyright Law, Section 110(1), 1976). This means that whether you purchased the video from a discount store or an educational compnay, whether it is marked

"For Home Use Only" or not, if it is for use in a teaching situation, you may use it without obtaining the permission of the video's owner. However, if you are using it for entertainment or reward, permission is needed. For more information on videos and copyright, see chapter 7: Videos, DVDs, CDs, and Copyright Law.

3. This does not replace the need to acquire permission, however.

4. Clearinghouse fees are typically dependent on the nature of the use the borrower requests.

5. For the purposes of this chapter, the various music clearinghouses are grouped together. There are three aspects to musical works: (1) sound recordings, which embody "the actual sound of the music," and which include all types of fixed sound recordings; (2) lyrics and sheet music, "the visual transcription of the words and music involved in the musical work," and (3) "musical sound that is part of a motion picture or audiovisual work" (Digilaw, 2000, 1). With these three aspects of musical works come a variety of licensing rights, among them: (1) mechanical rights, "the licensing of copyrighted musical composition records, tapes, and certain digital configurations" (Harry Fox Agency, 2004b, 1); and (2) digital licensing, "the licensing of copyrighted musical compositions in configurations, including but not limited to, full downloads, limited-use demand streaming and CD burning" (Harry Fox Agency, 2004a, 1). More on licensing is discussed in chapter 10: Music/Audio and Copyright Law.

REFERENCES

American Society of Composers, Authors and Publishers (ASCAP). 2003. New York: ASCAP. Available: www.ascap.com/licensing/about.html (accessed June 2, 2004).

———. 2004. "ASCAP Licensing: Frequently Asked Questions about Licensing." New York: ASCAP. Available: www.ascap.com/licensing/licensingfaq.html (accessed June 2, 2004).

Association of American Publishers. 2002. "How to Request Copyright Permission from Publishers." New York: Association of American Publishers. Available: www.publishers.org/about/higheredpermission.cfm (accessed June 7, 2004).

Bellingham Public Schools. 2003. "Copyright Permission Letter" Bellingham, WA: Bellingham Public Schools. Available: www.bham.wednet.edu/copyperm.htm (accessed June 2, 2004).

Broadcast Music, Inc. "BMI and Performing Rights." New York: Broadcast Music. Available: www.bmi.com/licensing/ (accessed June 7, 2004).

Bruwelheide, Janis H. 1995. *The Copyright Primer for Librarians and Educators*, 2nd ed. Chicago: American LibraryAssociation.

Butler, Rebecca P. 2001. "Obtaining Permission to Copy or Perform a Work, Part I." *Knowledge Quest* 30, no. 2 (November/December): 43–44.

———. 2002a. "Obtaining Permission to Copy or Perform a Work, Part II." *Knowledge Quest* 30, no. 3 (January/February): 32–33.

———. 2002b. "Obtaining Permission to Copy or Perform a Work, Part III." *Knowledge Quest* 30, no. 4 (March/April): 45–46.

Copyright Clearance Center (CCC). 2003. "Zip through Permissions as Never Before—Over the Web!" Danvers, MA: CCC. Available: www.copyright.com (accessed June 2, 2004).

DigiLaw. 2000. "Copyrighting Music." DigiLaw Publishing. Available: www.weblawresources.com/Copyright/copyrighting-music.htm (accessed June 7, 2004).

Fulcrum. n.d. "How to Apply for Permission." Seattle: University of Washington Copyright Connection. Available: http://fulcrumbooks.com/html/permissions.html (accessed June 2, 2004).

Harper, Georgia. 2001a. "Fair Use: Obtaining Permissions, Sample Letter Requesting Permission." Austin: University of Texas. Available: www.utsystem.edu/ogc/intellectualproperty/permmm.htm (accessed June 2, 2004).

———. 2001b. "Getting Permission." Austin: University of Texas. Available: www.utsystem.edu/ogc/intellectualproperty/permissn.htm (accessed June 2, 2004).

Harry Fox Agency. 2004. "Digital Licensing." New York: Harry Fox Agency. Available: www.harryfox.com/digital.html (accessed June 2, 2004).

———. 2004. "Mechanical Licensing." New York: Harry Fox Agency. Available: www.harryfox.com/mechanical.html (accessed June 2, 2004).

Illinois Association of School Boards. 1999. *General Personnel: Exhibit— Request to Reprint Material*. (February) 5.170–E: 1.

Innes, Catherine. 2000. "Requesting Permission." Seattle: University of Washington. Available: http://depts.Washington.edu/uwcopy/use/obtainingrights/5.shtml (accessed June 2, 2004).

Motion Picture Licensing Corporation. 2003. Los Angeles. Available: www.mplc.com/index2.htm (accessed June 2, 2004).

SESAC. 2003. "About SESAC." Nashville: SESAC. Available:

www.sesac.com/aboutsesac/aboutsesac1.html (accessed June 2, 2004).

Sholes, Carol. 2003. "Permission Guidelines." San Francisco: O'Reilly & Associates. Available: www.oreilly.com/oreilly/author/permission/ (accessed June 2, 2004).

Talub, Rosemary S. 2001. "Permissions, 'Fair Use,' and Production Resources for Educators and Librarians," Part I of II. *TechTrends* 45, no. 3 (May/June 2001): 8.

Templeton, Brad. 1995. "10 Big Myths about Copyright Explained." (April). Available: www.templetons.com/brad/copymyths.html (accessed June 2, 2004).

U.S. Copyright Law. 1976. Section 110. Washington, DC: Public Law 94-553.

Chapter Five

Other Important Copyright Issues: What Other Copyright Issues Do You Need to Know About?

INTRODUCTION

This chapter identifies a number of terms and issues concerning or related to copyright, and defines and discusses them in a general manner. Some of these subjects will be mentioned in subsequent chapters. Others, which are covered only in this chapter, will give you a larger context in which to place all copyright conversation.

DOCUMENTATION AND LICENSES

Documentation

The term documentation is used here to cover those informational and identifying records that each work possesses. As such, the documentation is, at least partially, that information usually found in the reference section of a paper. The examples used here are a print item, a Web item, and a piece of computer software. First, look at a book (print). The documentation for a book includes the author, title, copyright date, place of publication, publisher, and any special permissions that the copyright owner is willing to give the book owner or reader. Secondly, take a look at the Internet. Documentation for a Web site can vary somewhat from that for a print piece. It may also include the author, title, copyright date, place of publication, and publisher. In addition, it may include an e-mail link to the Webmaster or moderator of the site, the point of access to the site (URL), the date the site was last reorganized, agreements with which site users must abide, etc. The third example is computer software. Software documentation also includes such basic things as author/creator, title, copyright date, publisher, and place of publication. It usually also includes a copy of the contractual agreement (license—see below) between the purchaser of the software and the software seller. It is always best to read the documentation of any work from which you plan to borrow before doing any copying.

Licenses

A license is a "legally binding contract between two parties governing the use of an identified product or content for a specified purpose" (Torrans, 2003, 185). Licenses are very important in the world of copyright. For users, they define the ways that a protected (copyrighted) work can be used. The owner of the copyright uses the license to delineate which exclusive rights in a work are granted to others for their use. Keep in mind that the rights granted to the user are limited and nonexclusive, and they only extend to using the work for specified purposes. Normally licenses for works are automatically purchased with computer software, part of database documentation, involved in the rental of videos and DVDs, etc.[1] Essentially licenses are a part of the package that buyers purchase in conjunction with most works.[2] Suppose, for example, that your school purchases the license to place electronic publishing software on the computers in the English lab. The license is for 30 computers. If there are 31 computers in the lab, then legally either one computer may not have the software on its hard drive, or no more than 30 computers at a time may use the software, even if it is loaded on more than 30. Such actions depend on the contract between the purchaser and the seller.

Take another example: you, a biology teacher, bring the class to the library for research on a genetics unit. The library media specialist informs you that the school has purchased two database licenses from companies dealing in high school science. One database focuses on plant and animal genetics. With that particular license, your students may search the database and print out as many copies as they want of full-text articles on genetics. The second database also covers works focusing on plant and animal genetics. However, that license only allows users to print out one copy of any full-text article, without permission from the publisher. In each case, you need to follow the license directions. Even though the databases may be similar in format and subject areas, their licenses are not necessarily the same.

As a third example, let's suppose that you would like to use the video *Lorenzo's Oil* in your biology class. You feel that it will illustrate, in an understandable manner, some of the influences of genetics research. When you sign the form at the video rental store, you have essentially signed a license, or contract, and must abide by it. The form may be as simple as saying when the video must be returned. It could also include penalties for destroying or losing the video, returning it late, etc.

Remember, a license is contract law, not copyright law. If you are dealing with both a license and copyrighted material, you need to follow the licensing or contractual requirements first, because, "A license supersedes federal copyright law" (Martin, 2003).[3] Thus, when you obtain a license—a contract—to use a copyrighted work, you are essentially contracting to use certain copyrights afforded that work.

INTERLIBRARY LOAN

Like much of copyright law, those parts of the law that deal with interlibrary loan (ILL) can be very confusing. ILL, the borrowing of an item for use by another library, school, system, or individual who does not own that item, is a common occurrence in public and academic libraries. For K-12 school environments, ILL is an important way to obtain information not easily acquired by purchase. Usually ILL materials are those that a particular school cannot afford or does not often need. (Remember, if ILL is not available in your school, you can usually go to your local public library and request this service.)

In our swiftly evolving technological world, ILL has hit a new high— no longer do libraries need to send original items to their requestors via snail mail or paper copy. Now—with the help of scanners and the Internet—a copy of a requested material can be sent digitally.[4] Herein lies the rub. Copyright law can be violated by digital copying. Using the Internet, you obtain speed, easy access, and . . . possibly more copies than copyright law allows: the original paper copy (at the owner's library); the scanned copy (on the hard-drive of a computer in the owner's library); the digitized copy, which the requestor receives via the Internet; and the copy that the requestor prints out for ease of use. Now, instead of two copies, there is a minimum of four. When a library purchases an item, it purchases only that item, not the ability to copy it indiscriminately. While it is possible for the library to lend out its own copy, the creation of other copies may violate the agreement of the original item's purchase.

How do you get around this thorny issue and still have access to information and materials in a quick and easy manner? Take an article out of an obscure sports magazine as an example. Instead of borrowing the item via ILL, you could purchase the magazine issue in which the article is found, get a subscription to that magazine, or pay a fee to the copyright owner to have it copied. However, ILL is still a viable alternative. If you only want to borrow a copy, perhaps the lending library can send you the original. If borrowing it in a digital format is the viable alternative, you can encourage the lending library to immediately erase the scanned copy from its computer hard drive once the article has been sent, and upon receipt of the item, immediately print out a copy and erase the digitally received version from your hard-drive. Libraries may also have licenses to post articles on the Web or use specific databases. Sometimes, ILL can occur by accessing these sites through URLs.

It is important to mention the National Commission on New Technological Uses of Copyright Works (CONTU) Guidelines at this point, given the sports article example. Under Section 108(g)(2) of the copyright law of 1976, that part of the law covering "reproduction by libraries and archives" (U.S. Copyright Law, 1976), the lender is not allowed to send more than one copy of one article from a periodical issue. If more are sent, then the borrower must pay copyright fees. The CONTU Guidelines interpret Section 108(g)(2), and help librarians, copyright owners, and other interested parties in "understanding the amount of photocopying for use in interlibrary loan arrangements permitted under the copyright law" (CONTU, 1978). Under the CONTU Guidelines, borrowers may not receive more than *five* copies in *one year* from a *single* journal title published within the last *five years*. While the guidelines do not address nonjournal publications or material that is older than five years, they do give both the lenders (libraries and archives) and the borrowers some direction. An intended purpose of these guidelines is to discourage the use of ILL as a substitute for magazine subscriptions. In addition, when material is requested from a digital medium, licensing (see "Licenses" above and end note 1) may be involved (Martin, 2003).

Probably your easiest way to obtain your item via ILL is to go to your school library media specialist and ask for help. The library media specialist has been trained in such areas of access and can easily help you to obtain what you need in a timely manner with the minimum of copyright fuss (Butler, 2003).

STATUTORY EXEMPTIONS

If you search the U.S. Copyright Office Web site for statutory exemptions, you will find over two thousand of them. Not all of them, however, directly affect teachers and other school personnel. Nonetheless, there are some very important exemptions that do affect those directly (and indirectly) involved in K-12 education. First, though, it is helpful to define exactly what a statutory exemption is.

Definition

Statutory exemptions are written into the copyright law to provide some ways to use others' works without infringing on an owner's copyright and without needing to obtain permission to use a work. For example, fair use (see chapter 2) is a very important exemption, one that educators should definitely apply. Basically, with fair use, Congress tells us that there are certain ways that protected (copyrighted) works can be used for educational or research purposes while still protecting the owner's rights. There are a few other exemptions as well that are important to those in the K-12 environment, for example, exemption of certain performances and displays and reproduction by libraries and archives.

Limitations on Exclusive Rights: Exemption of Certain Performances and Displays

For educators, a very important statutory exemption to copyright law is section 110 of the 1976 U.S. Code (U.S. Copyright Law), "Limitations on exclusive rights: Exemption of certain performances and displays." This section of the copyright law covers exemptions in educational classroom settings and provides for the use of lawfully obtained copyrighted works in face-to-face instruction as well as in transmissions, under certain parameters. Use of the copyrighted works must be

- in a nonprofit educational institution;
- in a classroom or similar place of instruction;
- a performance or display that is a regular part of systematic instruction;
- a performance or display directly related to the teaching content; *and/or*
- for persons who are disabled or in special circumstances which otherwise prevent them from attending class (U.S. Copyright Law, sect. 110, 1976).[5]

Thus, under this exemption, a science teacher may play a recording of bird songs to his class, before the class goes on a field trip to a prairie restoration area, so that the students can recognize sounds of birds of the prairie.

Limitations on Exclusive Rights: Reproduction by Libraries and Archives

Another important statutory exemption for K-12 educators is found in section 108 of the 1976 copyright law: "Limitations on exclusive rights: Reproduction by libraries and archives." Section 108 talks about exemptions that are afforded libraries (for our purposes, school libraries and media centers) to copy works without violating copyright law. Section 108 provides that libraries may, within certain limits, make copies for preservation purposes, for private study, and for ILL. In order to do so, however, they must meet several requirements. These include:

- being open to the public or outside researchers,
- making copies that have no direct or indirect commercial advantage, and
- including a copyright notice on each copy made (or a statement that the work may be copyright protected, if there is no copyright notice on the original).

In most cases, the library can make only single copies. However, up to three copies can be made for purposes of:

- preservation and security;
- replacement of a lost, stolen, deteriorating, or damaged item; and
- changing the format of an obsolete work to one that can be used in the library (including, if the machine on which the format is played is obsolete) or an "unused replacement" is unavailable at a fair price (U.S. Copyright Law, 1976). (See Appendix III for the complete text of section 108.)

In addition, there are some limits under this exemption as to what libraries may and may not copy. While almost anything *may* be copied for preservation purposes, for purposes of ILL, or a researcher's needs, libraries *may not* copy the following types of works: audiovisual works, including motion pictures; musical works; and works such as pictures, graphs, and sculptures (Crews, 2000; U.S. Copyright Law, 1976, sec. 108). This means that libraries *may* copy for researchers or ILL "other types of works that are not specifically excluded (see list above); audio-visual works 'dealing with news' and pictures and graphics 'published as illustrations, diagrams, or similar adjuncts' to works that may otherwise be copied. (In other words, if you can copy the article, you can also copy the picture or chart that is in the article.)" (Crews, 2000, 83). These statutory exemptions are discussed in more detail in other parts of this book, where they affect copyright use of a certain work.

COPYING GUIDELINES

There are any number of congressional guidelines available for educators who need information on copyright. While these guidelines are not legal precedent, they can be helpful when trying to abide by copyright law. These classroom guidelines, which "have evolved from the principles codified in Copyright Act of 1976" (Torrans, 2003, 64), include those for:

- books and periodicals,
- music,
- off-air recordings,
- digital imaging,
- distance learning, and
- multimedia (see chapter 2).

The classroom guidelines are flexible; they provide a consertive definition for the use of works, *not the maximum* that the law permits. You actually could, in good faith, use more of a work than those conservative amounts suggest without infringing on the owners' copyright. Unfortunately, the maximum use is not clearly defined. Therefore, be aware, the further beyond the guidelines that you borrow from a work, the greater your chance of copyright infringement. If teachers and librarians follow the guidelines, they are considered to have acted in good faith. Because such guidelines have been enacted into legislation, however, they are not binding.

Schools often will choose to place a set (or several of the sets) of classroom guidelines in their schools' copyright and ethics policies because they are more understandable and definite than the law itself. Confusion arises when teachers, school librarians, technology coordinators, administrators, students, and others in the school understand the guidelines as if they were the maximum amounts allowable, rather than representing the more conservative approach. While using minimal amounts of works will guarantee that there will be no copyright infringements, it is also limiting to those who use, borrow, or copy materials for instructional purposes. Keep this in mind when the guidelines are referred to, for example, the "Multimedia Fair Use Guidelines" (chapter 2), the "Guidelines for Classroom Copying in Not-for-Profit Educational Institutions with Respect to Books and Periodicals" (chapter 12), and the appendices.

INTERNATIONAL COPYRIGHT LAW AND UNITED STATES COPYRIGHT LAW WITH INTERNATIONAL PROVISIONS

As if U.S. copyright law is not complicated enough, there is also international copyright law for you to be concerned with. While every country has its own laws in this area, which may or may not conform to our federal laws, there are some organizations to which we—and some other countries—belong. These organizations' treaties principally state that we will abide by the copyright laws of the other countries that have signed each treaty, and they will abide by ours. Several treaties, organizations, and acts that exist in this area, and of which the United States is a part, are discussed in this section. Two pieces of U.S. copyright law (the Digital Millenium Copyright Act and the Sonny Bono Copyright Extension Act) and database protection, another area of interest to educators, are also covered.

Universal Copyright Convention (UCC)

(International)
The United States joined the Universal Copyright Convention (UCC) on September 16, 1955. This group does not enforce copyright. Instead, it relies on its member nations to enforce its agreements (Besenjak, 1997; Bettig, 1996). A premise of the UCC is that its members must offer works from other participating countries the same copyright protection as those works created in their own country.

World Intellectual Property Organization (WIPO)

(International)
The World Intellectual Property Organization (WIPO) is a United Nations agency that "serves to protect the copyright laws of each signatory nation to the various treaties" (Torrans, 2003, 30). For example, in 1996, at a diplomatic conference in Geneva, Switzerland, the WIPO enacted two treaties dealing with international copyright law and digital communications. This organization is also the group that ruled that Time Warner would have sole ownership to Harry Potter–related Internet (domain) names (Kirkman, 1997; Neal, 2002; "Time Warner Gets 'Potter,'" 2000; Torrans, 2003).

Berne Convention for the Protection of Literary and Artistic Works

(International)
U.S. membership in the Berne Convention dates from March 1, 1989

(Besenjak, 1997). This international copyright treaty, signed by 96 countries, is the benchmark of all copyright agreements worldwide. It is administered by WIPO (Index Stock Imagery, 1996).[6]

Digital Millennium Copyright Act (DMCA)

(United States)
The DMCA, signed into law in October 1998 by President Clinton, made changes to U.S. copyright law in a number of areas, including online service provider liability, distance education, exemptions for libraries and archives, computer maintenance and copying of software, and digital performances of sound recordings. In addition, the DMCA implements the World Intellectual Property Organization treaties, thus bringing U.S. Copyright law into compliance with the WIPO. This was necessary because, while U.S. Copyright law met the standards of the WIPO treaties, it did not meet the treaties' prohibition on the picking of electronic locks used to protect online copyrighted works (Diotalevi, 1999; Peek, 1999; U.S. Copyright Office, 1998).[7] The DMCA provided this legislation.[8]

Sonny Bono Copyright Extension Act (CTEA)

(United States)
In an effort to maintain consistency between the United States and the other members of the Berne Convention, in 1998 Congress passed the Sonny Bono Copyright Term Extension Act (CTEA). So named because Congressman Bono was working on this at the time of his death, CTEA extends the duration of copyright in the United States retroactively from the life of the author plus fifty years to the life of the author plus seventy years and, in the case of works for hire and those under a corporate ownership, from seventy-five to ninety-five years or 120 years (whichever comes first) (Butler, 2003, 309).

Database Protection

(United States and International)
Database[9] protection is included in this section because of its importance to educators and the fact that changes in other countries' copyright laws affect it. On January 1, 1998, the European Union's Database Directive became effective. And as of March 2, 2004, there is a new version of database protection legislation in the United States House—H.R. 3872 (American Library Association, 2004; Scientific Access, 2002). What is database protection? In previous years, databases had one layer of protection under copyright law—to protect their "creativity or selection, coordination, and arrangement" (Webster, 2001). Under database

protection legislation, there is an additional type of protection—that of protecting the contents (facts) of the databases. With this in mind, many compilations currently in the public domain in the United States would become protected under copyright law. This issue is of special interest to educators and scientists. The way students and researchers could access information could be affected if they were at some point required to obtain permission to use, or pay for the use, of databases that until now have been in the public domain. Research could become more difficult—information harder to obtain and more expensive. Database protection is another area of interest to educators that bears watching in the future.

The purpose here is not to discuss the above issues in depth. Instead, it is to give an impression of selected items of importance occurring in this area. More specific information related to international copyright law, national legislation, and various works will be covered in chapters 6 through 14.

INFRINGEMENTS AND PENALTIES

Imagine that at a teacher's meeting after school, your principal asks you and your colleagues to stand if you think you have violated copyright law. If the group is truthful—and even half-way knowledgeable about copyright—it is likely that the whole room will stand. At this point, it is a common occurrence that at least one teacher will point out, "I copy all the time, and I've never been caught." Then a conversation will start about how schools and school districts don't have enough money, and that borrowing from sample textbooks, copying that extra workbook, using music off a popular CD for a multimedia presentation for the PTA, showing a rented video during a rainy recess, and so on, are okay because, "We're educators; we aren't going to earn any money off what we copy anyway." At this point the school library media specialist and technology coordinator may also speak up, asking, "Are we in trouble if we provide the equipment and software by which our teachers copy?" There are several misconceptions going on at this point that are worth looking at.

"Everyone in the Room Has Violated Copyright Law."

Because of the ambiguity in U.S. copyright law,[10] violating copyright law is easy to do. It may be a conscious or unconscious act.

Pretend that you are a computer teacher in an elementary school. You find a great piece of software that you are just positive will make learning keyboarding a quick and easy activity. Before you ask the technology coordinator to purchase a license for it, you want to try it out on a class. So . . . you copy it to all computers in your lab—even though you know that the documentation on the software says that this cannot be done without a license. Are you in violation of copyright law? Most definitely! (You are probably also in violation of contract law—see "Documentation and Licenses" in this chapter.) This is an example of conscious violation.

Assume that you are the middle school art teacher. Because of the popularity of the Harry Potter series, you decide that you will teach a unit on knitting, borrowing the idea of knitting hats for house elves that Hermione does in *Harry Potter and the Order of the Phoenix* (Rowling, 2003). You print out a pamphlet about knitting hats that you bought in a craft shop and hand it out to all of the students in your middle school classes. In your excitement to create this new assignment, you totally forget that such copying is in violation of copyright law: the pamphlet is not in the public domain, it doesn't fit under the fair use factors, and permission has not been granted. Have you violated copyright law? Most probably! This is an example of an unconscious act of violation.

"I'll Never Get Caught."

Well, you might not, but . . . Pretend that you are an exhausted kindergarten teacher. The kids have been running amok all week. It is now Friday afternoon, and all you want to do is get through the day. You can't take the students out for recess—it is raining hard, so you grab a Disney video from your book bag (you had rented it to show to your own children that night), pop it into the VCR, and sit back for a little badly needed rest. If you are cogent enough at this point to recognize that you are violating copyright law, you rationalize—the students are too young to realize that fact. Chances are that you are right—you will have a couple of hours of relative quiet and no one will be the wiser. But . . . now assume that one of your students, Ashley, has a father who works for the Disney Corporation. She goes home and proceeds to tell her family at the dinner table all about the movie that her class saw in school that day. Will you get caught? If Ashley's father decides to pursue the matter, you definitely could be found in copyright violation.[11] Now, on to another example.

"We Don't Have Enough Money to Buy Everything That We Need, So It's OK to Copy; After All, We're in Education."

Some educators feel that they should be able to copy or borrow from sources indiscriminately. This is because schools often do not have a lot of money for those extras that educators then feel they must purchase themselves. For instance, a teacher may find a sample workbook in a commercial teachers' store with an exercise that is perfect for a specific learning module. The teacher purchases the workbook, with full knowledge that each page of the book says that the material therein cannot be copied for classroom use. (One could ask then why such a workbook exists at all, but that is another discussion altogether.) The teacher, however, feels that since this is for an educational purpose, it is okay to copy the exercise for every student in the class. Unfortunately, the workbook's creator feels that every student in the class should own a workbook instead of the teacher's copying the exercise over and over from the one purchased copy. The creator has the right, under copyright law, to specify how the work is used. There are ways to obtain use of an owner's works by means of fair use, public domain, and permissions and licenses (see chapters 2 through 4), or possibly by statutory exceptions (see this chapter) or the "Guidelines for Classroom Copying" (also in this chapter). Therefore, the teacher is infringing, unless the copying fits under one of the above. Just being an educator or working with students in an educational setting does not mean that you can legally disregard copyright law.

"I Don't Violate Copyright Law. I Am in Charge of Equipment and Software That Is Used to Copy, However."

Assume that you are the school library media specialist. It is a small school, so you function as the technology specialist as well. All equipment, such as computers, VCRs, televisions, tape recorders, and the like, is under your jurisdiction. The same holds true for all software. A sixth-grade teacher comes in and sits down to use one of the lab computers. You pay no attention to him—he knows what he is doing, and you are busy with other things. Only later do you realize that he was burning a mix of songs from purchased CDs and Internet sources onto a CD for personal use. You recognize it is highly likely that this is in copyright violation. Should the teacher be caught for this act, would you also be held in violation for providing the instruments used for the copying? Unfortunately, you could be. This is an example of contributory or indirect infringement. "Anyone who knows or should have known that he or she is assisting, inducing or materially contributing to infringement of any of the exclusive rights by another person is liable for contributory infringement" (Simpson, 2001, 79).[12]

Penalties

Penalties for copyright infringements vary from fines to prison sentences. For example, in 2001, a Chicago suburban school was required to pay $50,000 to a computer association after it was discovered that a school employee had illegally downloaded software programs onto several school computers ("School District Pays…, 2001). Furthermore, I am unaware of any cases in which teachers have been imprisoned for copyright violation, but the penalties do exist in the U.S. Code (Title 17, sec. 506(a); Title 18, sec. 2319). An example of a video warning from *Independence Day* (1996) lists both a fine and jail time: The warning reads as follows:

> Federal law provides severe civil and criminal penalties for the unauthorized reproduction, distribution or exhibition of copyrighted motion pictures, video tapes or video discs. Criminal copyright infringement is investigated by the FBI and may constitute a felony with a maximum penalty of up to five years in prison and/or a $250,000 fine (*Independence Day*, 1996).

While this video warning is just an example of the kinds of warnings that are often placed on works, be aware that fines, sentences, and other penalties do exist, although they may vary from that of the *Independence Day* video. Why? The Copyright Law of the United States of America affords damages. As a consequence, there are ramifications for infringing on copyright law! Given some individuals' propensity towards using works indiscriminately, this is an issue to examine carefully.

At any given time, there are a number of bills and acts in the federal legislature concerned with copyright. Many of them are focused on increasing the fines or other penalties for disobeying the law.

PLAGIARISM

Plagiarism is when you borrow from another source without crediting the source or person from whom it was borrowed. Plagiarism can be intentional or unintentional. Intentional plagiarism is when someone purposely steals from another. For example, if you are an English teacher and one of your students knowingly copies a poem from a poetry anthology and turns it into you as his or her own, that student has intentionally plagiarized. Unintentional plagiarism occurs when someone does not cite (or does not properly cite) his or her sources. One instance of this might be if you, as a teacher, write an article for a professional journal. Because of sloppy note taking, you forget to cite one of the book chapters from which you obtained some of your information. The simplest ways to avoid plagiarizing are to not borrow indiscriminately and to cite your sources (Harris, 2002).

Copyright is not directly related to plagiarism. However, the two are often associated with one another.[13] Perhaps this is because both involve copying materials.[14] It is possible to both break copyright law and plagiarize (Harris, 2002). A case in point would be if Mr. Brown, a computer teacher, decides to take a chapter from a book detailing a presentation software and claim it as his own on a personal Web site. Assuming that the book is not in the public domain, if he does not ask for permission to use the chapter and borrows more than fair use allows, he violates copyright law. Putting the name "Brown" on something he did not write is an example of plagiarism. Thus, Mr. Brown manages to both violate copyright law and plagiarize.[15] Be aware, however, that citing sources does not mean that it is permissible to violate copyright law.

How to Cite

"Overcitation is never a vice; undercitation is never a virtue" (Harris, 2002, 22). As Harris states here, it is better to cite something that you have borrowed than risk plagiarizing. How to cite what you borrow is another issue, one that is not within the scope of this book. However, there are any number of citation styles, some of the most common coming from the American Psychological Association (APA), the Modern Language Association (MLA), and the *Chicago Manual of Style*.[16] Manuals of style can be found in a number of places: online on college and university sites, some K-12 school sites, other Web sites, and for sale in commercial bookstores.[17] While correctly citing material borrowed is an important skill to have when authoring any intellectual work, its relationship to copyright is only peripheral: "…copying even a small amount of an earlier work can be plagiarism, to be copyright infringement the copying must be substantial in either quantity or quality" (Stearns, 1999, 10).

SAMPLE FLOW CHART

Figure 5.1 is an example of the flow charts that are used in part II of this book to respond to copyright questions that have more than one answer. Read through each diagram in chapters 6 through 14, from top to bottom to obtain the answers to the questions posted above all flow charts. Remember, when you use the flow charts in this book, you are trying to find any criterion under which you may borrow a work. Therefore, you need only to follow each flow chart until you come to that point where you satisfy one of the criteria. Once you reach that point, there is no need to go any further.

Figure 5–1
Sample Flow Chart

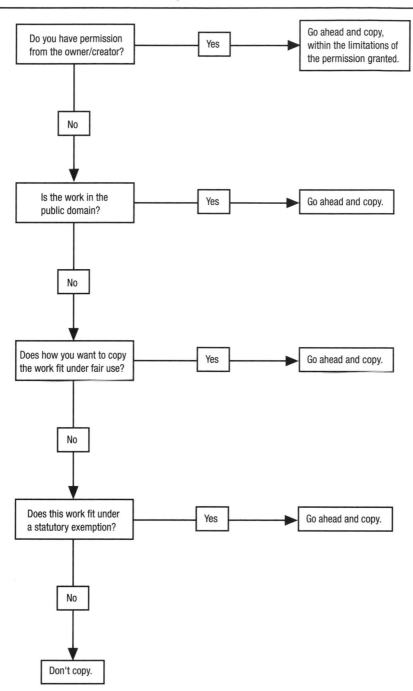

CONCLUSION

This chapter looks at a number of copyright-related items, including documentation and licenses, interlibrary loan, statutory exemptions for educators and librarians, and classroom copying guidelines. It also addresses international copyright law and ways the United States has chosen to add to its own laws to comply with international copyright treaties, copyright infringements in K-12 schools, educators' attitudes towards such infringements, and the penalties for copyright violations, which you need to be aware of. Although not directly related to copyright law, plagiarism and correct citing styles are also part of this chapter. This is because many educators associate these topics with copyright. Finally, there is a sample of the flow charts used in part II and an explanation.

Now that you have an idea about a variety of issues that come into play when you are applying copyright law to works in a variety of formats, it is time to turn to the practical application of copyright in the K-12 school setting.

END NOTES

1. A common type of computer software license is what is called the "shrink-wrap license." This type of license gets its name "from the clear plastic wrapping that encloses many software packages. They contain a notice that by tearing open the shrink-wrap, the user assents to the software terms enclosed within" (Kunkel, 2002, 3). Shrink-wrap licenses usually include such things as an agreement notice, transfer and modification restrictions, bans on reverse engineering, copyright information, etc. (Kunkel, 2002). There are also licenses, found on the Web, which are becoming more common. One is the "clickwrap license." "Clickwrap agreements came into use when software vendors began distributing software by means other than disks, such as when the software is pre-installed on a computer for the user, or when the software is downloaded over the Internet. Upon downloading, installation or first use of the application, a window containing the terms of the license opens for the user to read. The user is asked to click either 'I agree' or 'I do not agree.' If the user does not agree, the process is terminated" (Kunkel, 2002, 8). Another type of license found on the Web is the "browsewrap license." "Browsewrap agreements do not appear on the screen and the user is not compelled to accept or reject the terms as a condition of proceeding with further computer opera-

tions. Instead, a browsewrap agreement appears only as a hyperlink that is accessed by clicking on the link. It is optional, not required" (Kunkel, 2002, 11). There are several differences between clickwrap and browsewrap agreements. While the user is notified up front of all agreement terms with clickwrap, the user may or may not know the terms of the browsewrap license—depending on whether or not he or she has made the decision to link to the "terms and conditions" page. Next, the user must acknowledge agreement to the terms of the license with the clickwrap agreement. That is not true with the browsewrap license, where the user may not even know what the terms or conditions of the agreement are. Last, the user is definitely aware of having agreed to certain terms with the clickwrap license. With the browsewrap license, the user may not even realize that he or she has agreed to a contract (Kunkel, 2002).

2. Licensing information is most often located near the front or beginning of a work's documentation. It is usually in fine print, and, often, online it can be something that the user can quickly click away. Be sure to read this fine print—you may be signing away rights that you need.

3. Licenses are copyright information (see chapters 4 and 6 through 14 for more information).

4. Interlibrary loan (ILL), in the original sense, was about distributing material, not copying. Digital ILL is concerned with both.

5. The TEACH Act of 2002 amends Section 110(2) by adding films and other dramatic works to the exemption, and also by redefining the terms of use by nonprofit educational institutions of copyrighted materials in distance education, including Web courses (Campos, 2002; Crews, 2002). However, you and your school must abide by all of the TEACH Act's requirements in order to use this additional exemption. (See more on the TEACH Act in chapter 13: "Distance Learning and Copyright Law.")

6. More international agreements that focus on intellectual properties include the General Agreement on Trade and Tariffs (GATT) and the Trade-Related Aspects of Intellectual Property Rights (TRIPS) agreement (Bettig, 1996).

7. Electronic locks are technological copy protection devices used to "lock" computer code (Lemos, 2001).

8. In actuality, while the DMCA does implement the World Intellectual Property Organization (WIPO) treaties, it also "creates two new prohibitions in Title 17 of the U.S. Code (1976 Copyright Law)—one on circumvention of technological measures used by copyright

owners to protect their works and one on tampering with copyright management information—and adds civil remedies and criminal penalties for violating the prohibitions" (DMCA, 1998, 2). Libraries and other concerned groups are worried that, by going beyond the WIPO treaties, the DMCA is pushing the envelope in regard to fair use. This is an area for educators to be cautious about in the future.

9. A database is "an organized body of related information" (WordNet, n.d.). Databases can be in many formats; however, today we usually think of them in terms of information stored, retrieved, and accessed via computer. Telephone books are an example of a database currently in the public domain.

10. Because copyright law has the dual function of representing two diverse groups, owners and users, it has been a vague law from its very inception in the U.S. Congress (Lawrence and Timberg, 1989).

11. More on copyright and videos is found in chapter 7: Videos, DVDs, and Copyright Law. More on how to deal with those who violate, how and why to respect copyright law, and related topics is found in chapter 14.

12. There are three kinds of infringement: (1) direct, in which a user violates the rights of the owner or author by making illegal copies or derivatives of copyrighted works, distributing these copies/derivations, or publicly performing or displaying the works; (2) contributory, in which an individual or group is aware that what they are doing assists another in copyright infringement; and (3) vicarious, where those with authority over an infringer gain benefits from the infringement (Simpson, 2001).

13. "Cases of literary plagiarism most often turn up in court as cases of copyright infringement" (Stearns, 1999, 8).

14. Historically copyright and plagiarism are also linked. In England, the eighteenth century is noted for the first copyright statutes as well as a strong concern about plagiarism (Mallon, 1989).

15. ". . . the legal status of a piece of information has no bearing on whether or not it needs to be cited" (Harris, 2002, 21).

16. Web pages and other items posted online are especially confusing to cite and vary from style manual to style manual. Below are citation styles used by APA, MLA, the *Chicago Manual of Style*, and Turabian to cite an Internet site.

    APA: Author; publication date; title of work; retrieval month, day and year; source (URL) (APA, 2003).

    MLA: Author; title of work; document date (if different from access date); access date source (URL) (Gibaldi, 2003).

Chicago Manual of Style: Author/editor; date of publication; title of work; source description (is it a home page, online journal article, etc.); place of publication; publisher; access date: day, month, and year; source (URL); format (Internet is usually identified here as the citation medium) (*Chicago Manual of Style*, 2003).

Turabian: Author; title; place of publication; publisher; date of publication; source description (is it a home page, online journal article, data base, etc.); source (URL); access date (Turabian, 1996).

17. There are also other Web sites that provide information on citation, such as NoodleTools, an Internet site of "interactive tools designed to aid students and professionals with their online research" (NoodleTools, 2004, 1).

18. In addition to the criteria in the flow charts, it is possible that some statutory exemptions, such as those for either educational classroom settings or those for reproductions by libraries and archives, may apply. See the section on statutory exemptions in this chapter.

REFERENCES

American Library Association. 2004. "Database Protection Legislation." Chicago: American Library Association. (April) Available: www.ala.org/ala/washoff/WOissues/copyrightb/dbprotection/databaseprotection.htm (accessed June 8, 2004).

American Psychological Association (APA). 2003. "APA Style.org: Electronic References." Washington, DC: American Psychological Association. Available: www.apastyle.org/elecmedia.html (accessed June 7, 2004).

Besenjak, Cheryl. 1997. *Copyright Plain & Simple*. Franklin Lakes, NJ: Career Press.

Bettig, Ronald. 1996. *Copyrighting Culture: The Political Economy of Intellectual Property*. Boulder, CO: Westview.

Butler, Rebecca P. 2003. "Copyright and Organizing the Internet." *Library Trends* 52, no. 2 (Fall): 307–317.

Campos, Carol. 2002. "Recent Copyright Law Developments for Distance Education: The TEACH Act." Boston: Holland & Knight LLP. (December). Available: www.hklaw.com/Publications/Newsletters.asp?ID=332&Article=1856 (accessed June 7, 2004).

The Chicago Manual of Style, 15th ed. 2003. Chicago: University of Chicago Press. Electronic edition available at www.press.uchicago.edu/Misc/Chicago/cmosfaq/tools.html (accessed June 8, 2004).

CONTU. 1978. Final Report of the National Commission on New Technological Uses of Copyrighted Works. "CONTU Guidelines on Photocopying under Interlibrary Loan Arrangements." Washington, DC: Library of Congress. (July). Available: www.cni.org/docs/infopols/ CONTU.html (accessed June 7, 2004).

Crews, Kenneth D. 2000. *Copyright Essentials for Librarians and Educators*. Chicago: American Library Association.

———. 2002. "The Technology, Education and Copyright Harmonization (TEACH) Act." Chicago: American Library Association. Available: www.ala.org/washoff/teach.html (accessed June 7, 2004).

Digital Millennium Copyright Act (DMCA). 1988. Public Law No. 105-304, 112 stat. 2860 (October 28).

Diotalevi, Robert N. 1999. "Copyright Law and Policy for the Digital Millennium Educator." *WebNet Journal* 1, no. 4 (October-December): 44–46.

Gibaldi, Joseph. 2003. *MLA Handbook for Writers of Research Papers*, 6th ed. New York: Modern Language Association.

Harris, Robert A. 2002. *Using Sources Effectively: Strengthening Your Writing and Avoiding Plagiarism*. Los Angeles: Pyrczak.

Independence Day. 1996. Produced by Centropolis Entertainment. 145 min. Twentieth Century Fox. Videocassette.

Index Stock Imagery. 1996. "Understanding the Berne Convention." New York: Index Stock Imagery. Available: www.indexstock.com/pages/ berne.htm (accessed June 7, 2004).

Kirkman, Catherine Sansum. 1997. "The WIPO Copyright Treaty." San Francisco: CMP Media. (July) Available: www.webtechniques.com/ archives/1997/07/just/ (accessed June 7, 2004).

Kunkel, Richard G., JD. 2002. "Recent Developments in Shrinkwrap, Clickwrap and Browsewrap Licenses in the United States." Perth, Australia: Murdoch University Electronic Journal of Law. (September). Available: www.murdoch.edu/au/elaw/issues/v9n3/kunkel93_text.html (accessed May 6, 2004).

Lawrence, John Shelton, and Bernard Timberg, eds. 1989. *Free Use and Free Inquiry: Copyright Law and the New Media*, 2nd ed. Norwood, NJ: Ablex.

Lemos, Robert. 2001. "Protesters Declare War on Copyright Law." San Francisco: ZDNet News. (August). Available: www.newbusinessnews .com/story/08300101.html (accessed June 7, 2004).

Mallon, Thomas, 1989. *Stolen Words: The Classic Book on Plagiarism*. New York: Harcourt.

Martin, Rebecca. 2003. "The Library: Copyright and Licensing." Classroom handout at Northern Illinois University, DeKalb, IL.

Neal, James G. 2002. "Copyright is Dead . . . Long Live Copyright." *American Libraries* 33, no. 11 (December): 48–51.

"NoodleTools—Smart Tools, Smart Research." 2004. Palo Alto, CA: NoodleTools. Available: http://noodletools.com/ (accessed June 7, 2004).

Peek, Robin. 1999. "Taming the Internet in Three Acts." *Information Today* 16, no. 1 (January): 28–29.

Rowling, J. K. 2003. *Harry Potter and the Order of the Phoenix*. New York: Scholastic Press.

"School District Pays Copyright Penalty." 2001. *Chicago Tribune*, October 12, sec. 2, 3.

Simpson, Carol. 2001. *Copyright for Schools: A Practical Guide*, 3rd ed. Worthington, OH: Linworth.

Stearns, Laurie. 1999. "Copy Wrong: Plagiarism, Process, Property, and the Law." In *Perspectives on Plagiarism and Intellectual Property in a Postmodern World*, eds. Lisa Buranen and Alice M. Roy, 5–17. Albany: State University of New York Press.

"Time Warner Gets 'Potter.'" 2000. *Chicago Tribune*. December 29, sec. 5, 8.

Torrans, Lee Ann. 2003. *Law for K-12 Libraries and Librarians*. Westport, CT: Libraries Unlimited.

Turabian, Kate. 1996. *A Manual for Writers of Term Papers, Theses, and Dissertations*. 6th ed. Chicago: University of Chicago Press.

U.S. Copyright Law. 1976. Public Law 94-553, sec. 108,110.

U.S. Copyright Office, Library of Congress. 1998. *The Digital Millennium Copyright Act of 1998: U.S. Copyright Office Summary*. Washington, D.C.: U.S. Copyright Office.

Webster, Ferris. 2002. "Scientific Access to Data and Information: A Summary of Database Protection Activities." Newark: University of Delaware. (February). Available: www.codata.org/data_access/summary.html (accessed June 7, 2004).

WordNet. n.d. "Overview for 'database.'" Princeton, NJ: WordNet 2.0. Available: www.cogsci.princeton.edu/cgi-bin/webwn?stage=1&word=database (accessed June 8, 2004).

Part II

Specific Applications of Copyright Law

Chapter Six

The Internet and Copyright Law: Everything on the Web Is Considered Implied Public Access, Right?

INTRODUCTION

Activities such as sending e-mail, using the World Wide Web as an information tool, creating Web pages, linking to other Web sites, and the like, may open the possibility of violating copyright law, whether you realize it or not. Because the Internet is a relatively new phenomenon, the question—how should you protect yourself and your students as you explore this exciting communication realm—is a common one.[1]

This chapter addresses questions that cover the Internet and a variety of copyright issues. Questions with more than one answer are presented in flow chart form. Remember, when you use the flow charts in this chapter, you are trying to find any criterion under which you may borrow a work. Therefore, you need only follow each flow chart until you come to that point where you satisfy one of the criteria. Once you reach that point, there is no need to go any further. Additionally, for more information on each area discussed, please refer to the chapter (chapters 1 through 5) that covers that particular subject. Also, use the index and table of contents for more material on the topic that interests you.

FAIR USE

Question: Is there fair use on the Internet?

Figure 6–1
Web Images

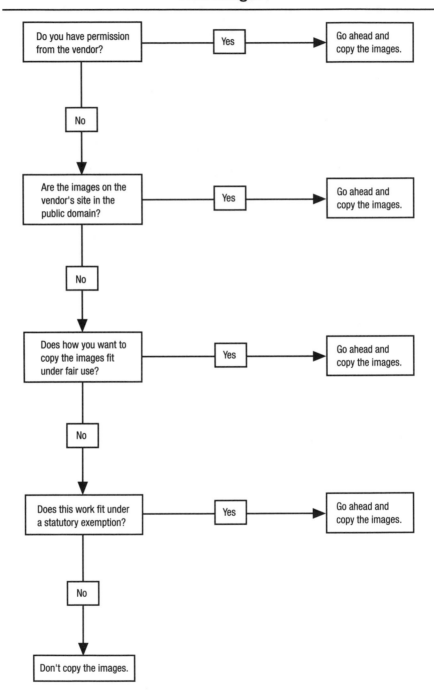

Answer: While U.S. copyright laws are still catching up when it comes to Internet usage, it is best to apply fair use to Web sites, e-mails, and all other electronic communications.

Question: Can school library media specialists use images from online booksellers or other vendor sources to promote books and other media on their own library Web sites?

Answer: Since vendors are in the business of making money, it is likely they would not mind their images existing on your site to promote those things that they sell. However, since images on vendor sites can be copyrighted, please consult the flow chart in Figure 6-1 before putting an image on your Web site.

Question: A friend e-mailed me a copy of a joke. Can I send it on to others or post it on a listserv with no repercussions?

Answer: To have a copy does *not* mean you have a copyright. If the joke was sent to you and there is no documentation attached, assume it is under copyright and do not send it on without permission of the original owner. However, you may discuss it or send parts of it under the fair use factors.

Question: Can I print off a Web page and make a copy of it for every student in my class?

Answer: Use the flow chart in Figure 6-2 to determine what is allowed.

Question: I want to copy several paragraphs from a site on pyramids. How much may I borrow from someone's Web page under the fair use factors?

Answer: The amount you may copy is based on the total amount of material on the site, how much you want to borrow, whether it is the heart of the work or not, whether it is fact or fiction, published or unpublished, whether such borrowing will affect the marketplace, and how you are going to use what you borrow (see chapter 2). "When you claim fair use, you take a risk. The wording of fair use language in the Copyright Act is vague and subject to interpretation by the courts!" (Besenjak, 1997, 58).

Question: I found a great photograph of Mark Twain on a college Web page. I want to use it for my eighth-grade advanced-literature Internet site. However, the college does not answer my queries. Is it all right to use the photograph anyway?

Figure 6–2
Printing Web Pages

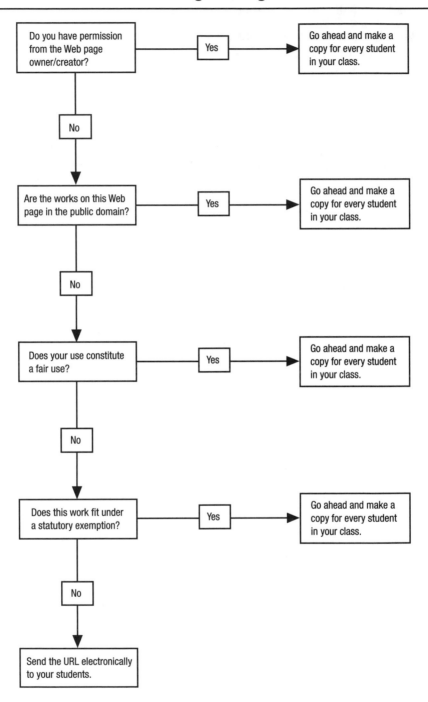

Figure 6–3
Photographs on the Web

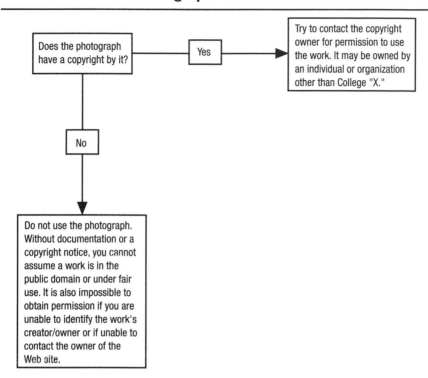

Answer: Use the flow chart in Figure 6-3 to decide if it is all right to use the photograph.

PUBLIC DOMAIN

Question: Is the Internet in the public domain?

Answer: The Internet is "a global information system of linked addresses to support communication . . . an infrastructure . . ." (Debbie Abilock, Sept. 1, 2003, personal e-mail communication). Web pages' content, e-mail, and other electronic communications that make up the Internet can be copyrighted. If the content of any Web page is in the public domain, it *should* say so somewhere on the site. (*Should* is an operative word here—the site owner or administrator does not *have* to state whether Internet content is copyrighted.) However, if there is no statement either way, one should assume that the Web page content is copyrighted.

Figure 6–4
Deep Linking

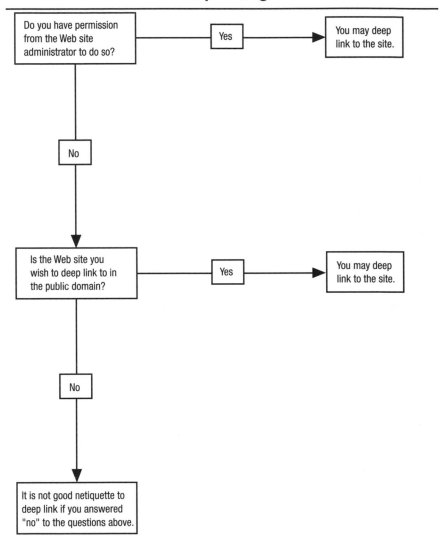

DOCUMENTATION AND LICENSES

Question: Where is the documentation located on a Web page?

Answer: Documentation (that information in most works that states the work's identifying data, such as author, copyright date, publisher, place of publication, etc.) on a Web page is usually at the beginning or end of the site. It may be as simple as listing the Webmaster or moderator of the site and when the site was last updated. Documentation can also include permissions or restrictions to which the user of the site must agree, copyright information, and other criteria that the moderator or owner of the site has determined must be met for site usage (see chapter 5). Please remember to read all documentation before agreeing to or checking off on a site. It is to your advantage to know that to which you have agreed.

Question: Do K-12 educators need to be concerned with licenses for Web access?

Answer: In most school situations, licenses are either the responsibility of the technology coordinator and apply to the number of computers that can use a particular piece of software at one time or in a particular manner, or the responsibility of the librarian and apply to online databases (Hoffmann, 2001) or access to other online information sources, such as online encyclopedias. However, while the classroom teacher may not hold primary responsibility for computer licenses (software) and Web access (online databases/ online encyclopedias) in that such responsibilities are someone else's job, the teacher needs to be knowledgeable about the terms of licenses, should know and abide by these terms, and should ensure that the students do the same. In addition, there is always the possibility that a classroom teacher will request a specific Web site for which a license is required and for which neither the technology coordinator or school librarian is accountable. In such an instance, the license could become the responsibility of the classroom teacher.

PERMISSIONS

Question: I am a physical education teacher. Do I need permission to link my school Web page on soccer to a general sports page?

Answer: No, such linking is usually considered a public domain concept.[2] However, it is good "Netiquette" (Internet etiquette) to ask the owner of the general page if you may link to his or her Web site.

Question: May I make a deep link to a school-related site without permission?[3]

Answer: Use the flow chart in Figure 6–4 to make your decision.

Some copyright experts and users argue that linking is an address, similar to cross-references in a library catalog. As such, linking (including deep linking) cannot be copyrighted. Others disagree,

Figure 6–5
Copying Lists

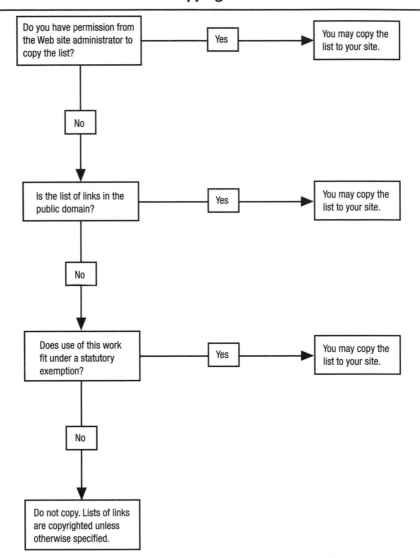

saying that linking (especially deep linking, which can bypass advertising pages) may infringe on a copyright owner's rights (Delio, 2002; Dorr, Gray, and Holcomb, 2002; Ricciuti, 1997; Ruse, 2000; Simpson, 2001; Templeton, n.d.). While at the present there is no legal precedent to claim that deep linking infringes on copyright, to avoid the risk of lawsuits and "cease and desist" letters, it may be easier not to deep link. (See Figure 6-4.)

Figure 6–6
Borrowing All or Parts of Web Pages

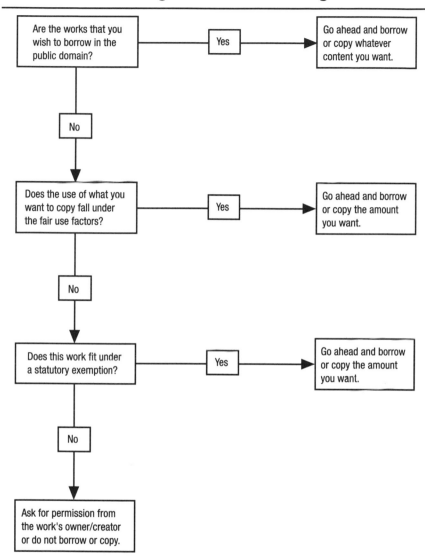

Question: May I copy a list of links about birds of North America that I found on an ornithology site to my eighth-grade class's science Web page?

Answer: Use the flow chart in Figure 6-5 to decide if you may copy the list.

Question: Do I need special permission from Internet authors to borrow or copy parts or all of their Web pages?

Answer: Use the flow chart in Figure 6-6 to make your decision.

Question: Do I need permission to link my Web page to other authors' Web pages?

Answer: No. However, it is good netiquette to do so.

YOU CREATE IT, YOU OWN IT

Question: Is it a copyright infringement if someone takes an e-mail you sent and posts it on a listserv? (Imagine that you sent an e-mail out to a group of students. You have information vital to an algebra assignment that you wish them to read before the next class. The information is a piece that you created yourself, just for this class. You attach it to the e-mail and send it out. Weeks later, a teacher at another school tells you that he received a forwarded copy of your work from a student at your school. He says that he received it from a math listserv. You are incensed; you did not give permission for this piece to be forwarded to any others. This particular information was for your class only. A copy forwarded to a listserv means that potentially thousands of people you do not know now have your work.

Answer: The answer to this question is a resounding "yes." Anything you create—and this includes other formats of works as well—is immediately copyrighted, whether you officially register it with the U.S. Copyright Office or not (Howie, 1997). Thus, whoever sent it to the listserv (since you did not give your permission) is in violation of copyright law. In addition, those on the listserv who keep and use your work may also be in violation.

Question: Who owns the copyright to a Web page you created for your fourth-grade class, if you worked on it at home in the evenings and used your own computer and software?

Answer: If you worked on this Web page, using your own equipment and software, and all on your own time, then it should be yours, provided you did not sign an agreement with your school that said otherwise. If you worked on it at school, using only school equipment and software, and on school time, then chances are that it comes under "work for hire."[4] If you created it partly at home and partly at work, then who owns it becomes more complicated. Some school systems have contractual agreements with their employees or policies that cover this issue. These policies vary in identifying the owner of the work. In this case, check with your school system regulations.[5]

INFRINGEMENTS AND PENALTIES

Question: Is file swapping an infringement of copyright law?

Answer: File swapping, "downloading copyrighted music online" (CNET News, 2002), is an issue that probably exists more in homes than in the educational environment. However, because it is so popular, it is addressed briefly here. File swapping is an infringement of copyright law, since it involves the sharing of music files from one computer to another, (1) without obtaining permission from the music's original owners/producers and (2) without following the fair use factors. Recording companies are angry, ordinary citizens are being sued (Electric Frontier Foundation, 2003; Lambert et al., 2003; CNET News, 2003), and even popular magazines like *Reader's Digest* (RD Technology, 2003) and *People* (Lambert et al., 2003) feature stories about this issue. Even more confusing to the ordinary populace is that software, such as that produced by Grokster and StreamCast for the purpose of downloading music, may be considered legal (CNET News, 2002)! Thus, you can purchase file swapping software, but if you use it in the way it is intended to be used, then you have violated copyright law! (This is similar to the copying of videos, computer software, and other works that we will discuss in future chapters. While the equipment and software needed to copy works are usually legal, the actual act of copying such works without permission may not be legal.)

Question: What are the penalties for copyright infringement involving file swapping?

Answer: The penalties and effects for file swapping, when it is considered a copyright infringement,[6] include:

- up to $150,000 in fines for each downloaded song,
- lawsuits,
- cease and desist letters,
- turning off file-sharing software,
- criminal prosecutions,
- jail sentences, and
- lectures and college orientations on the legalities and illegalities of down-loading (Electronic Frontier Foundation, 2003; Lambert et

al., 2003; National Association of College Stores [NACS], 2003;
CNET News, 2003).

Question: Is copying off the Internet (electronically or in print) an
infringement of copyright law? If so, what are the penalties?

Answer: Use the flow chart in Figure 6-7 to decide if the copying
you want to do is legal according to copyright law. Use the same
three criteria in Figure 6-7 to decide if you can legally send material by e-mail. Sending material from another source via e-mail can
be an infringement.

Penalties for Internet infringements are varied at present. Potential ramifications of infringement include receiving a "cease and
desist" letter;[7] lawsuits, which might include court-ordered payment
of damages plus any profits from the copyright misuse to the copyright owner(s); and payment of fines (usually at a judge's discretion) (Hoffmann, 2001). Because the Internet is such a new source
for copyright registrations, there have been very few legal actions
thus far. It is very likely that in the future the courts will decide
the outcomes of such infringements.

Question: Is framing an infringement of copyright law?

Answer: Framing, essentially the ability of a user to view more than
one Web page in a browser window (Hoffmann, 2001), is a very
gray issue when it comes to copyright. Because framing can be seen
as creating a derivative work, such use might be considered an infringement. Currently there is no real answer to this question.
Therefore, the moderate response would be either to avoid framing or use it sparingly.

INTERNATIONAL COPYRIGHT LAW

Question: What if your class is studying religions around the world.
One of your students finds an excellent site on the Druids. However, the site comes from another country. Do we need to be concerned with international copyright law when we use the Internet?

Answer: While the U.S. belongs to a number of conventions and
treaties designed to bring copyright laws worldwide into line (see
chapter 5), in fact, there is no one copyright law in the world. Each
country has its own laws. However, under the Berne Convention,
the idea is that the member nations must treat the works of non-

Figure 6–7
Copying Off the Internet

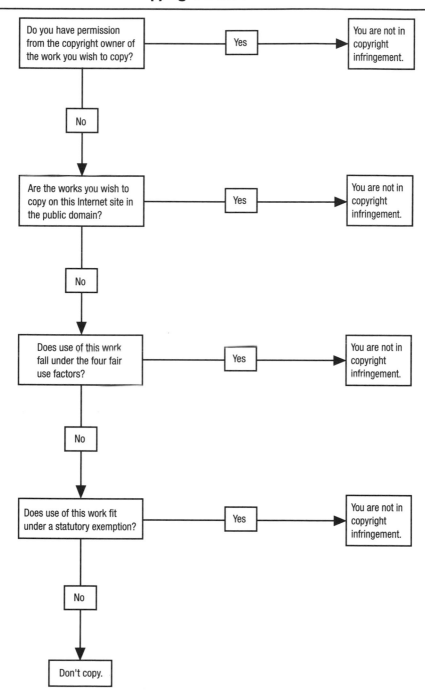

citizens the same as they would protect the works of their own citizens. This means that laws that apply to works created in the United States should also apply to works created in other countries—no matter what the format (Yu, 2001). Thus, when you use Web pages from other countries, you are safest—copyright-wise —if you treat the Web pages as if they had been created in the U.S.[8]

AVOIDING COPYRIGHT PROBLEMS

Question: May I borrow material from an algebra Web site to place on a math site I am creating for my class? Do I need to cite the owner/creator of the work I want to borrow?

Answer: Sometimes the owner of a borrowed work just wants credit for the work. This means that if you are creating a Web page or posting to the Web, and you want to borrow from a site (or another work) to do so, you should ask the owner/creator of the material for permission to use his or her work (unless your borrowing comes under the fair use factors or public domain). Then, on your Web page, put in a reference crediting the owner/creator of the work that you borrowed. This reference can be at either the beginning or the end of your Web page or at the point of the citation itself. Failure to cite a work, besides making an owner/creator angry, is also plagiarism.[9] So when you borrow *anything*, cite! (Remember: plagiarism is *different* from copyright infringement. You can cite the owners for something you have copied and still be infringing on their copyright.)

Question: How do database licenses work?

Answer: Read the license (usually) located at the beginning of the database (often you are required to click out of it before you can go further into the database). It will tell you what you can copy, print off, and what you can't. Some databases let you print out whole articles. Others allow you to search but not print, unless you have purchased a site license. Since database rights vary one to another, make sure that you are aware of exactly what rights you have with each one. There are certain things you should remember about databases, licenses, and copyright:

- Licenses may be more restrictive than fair use; however, when you agree to the license, it is a legal contract and you must abide by it.
- Database material may or may not be from copyrighted publications.

- "Click-on" licenses on the Internet are nonnegotiated contracts. Because of this, there is currently dissent as to whether or not "clicking away certain copyrights" is actually legal.
- Database collections are not protected by U.S. copyright law (Torrans, 2003).

CONCLUSION

It's challenging to be a K-12 educator—especially in the age of electronic communications and the confusion over that very vague set of laws called copyright. The three most important questions to ask when borrowing/ using another's electronic works are:

- Does what I want to borrow fit under the fair use factors?
- Is what I want to borrow in public domain?
- Can I obtain permission to use all or part of this work from the owner/author?

END NOTES

1. Those who originally wrote U.S. copyright law perceived ownership in terms of print works (Bettig, 1996).
2. This is true for most links. One exception is if the format of the link itself could be copyrighted, such as that of a copyrighted image.
3. "Deep linking refers to connecting to a specific page buried within a site, rather than the site's homepage" (Hoffmann, 2001, 59).
4. Section 201(b) of the Copyright Law of the United States talks about work made for hire. It states, "In the case of a work made for hire, the employer or other person for whom the work was prepared is considered the author for purposes of this title, and, unless the parties have expressly agreed otherwise in a written instrument signed by them, owns all of the rights comprised in the copyright" (U.S. Copyright Law, 1976). What this means is that, "when an employee has created a work within the scope of his employment, the work is considered a "work made for hire," and the employer—not the creator—owns the work" (Howie, 1997, 19).
5. Like so much dealing with copyright, there are a number of factors to consider when determining who owns what, such as where, when, and how the work was created. For example, the U.S. Supreme Court ruling in 1989 on the *Community for Creative Non-Violence (CCNV) v. Reid* is such a case (U.S. Supreme Court, 1989).

In brief, this case considers who owns the copyright to a statue: the artist (Reid) who created the statue in his studio after a verbal agreement with the CCNV, or the CCNV, which commissioned it. First, a district court ruled in favor of CCNV, holding that it was "work made for hire." However, a Court of Appeals reversed that decision, stating that it was not within the scope of employment for Reid given that he was an independent contractor under agency law, and that the agreement for the statue as a "work made for hire" had not been in writing. The opinion of the U.S. Supreme Court, delivered by Justice Marshall on June 5, 1989, was that it was not "work for hire," since Reid was an independent contractor rather than an employee of the CCNV. In delivering this decision, multiple factors were considered by the court. These same factors could be applied by other courts determining who owns the copyright to material on a Web site, should such ever become a lawsuit. The factors to be considered are (1) determining whether a work is created by an employee (work made for hire) within the definition of the 1976 copyright law, Section 101(1) or (2) by an independent contractor within the definition of the 1976 copyright law, Section 101(2); or that of (3) joint authorship, thus copyright co-ownership under Section 201(a) of the Copyright Law of 1976 (U.S. Copyright Law, sec. 101(1), 101(2), 201(a); U.S. Supreme Court, 1989).

6. File swapping does not always constitute an infringement.
7. A "cease and desist" letter is, in simple terms, a letter sent by an individual or group's attorneys when works owned by the individual or group are being used without permission. The letter, typically written in an aggressive tone, demands that the infringing party respect the owner's copyright and stop using the works. As a rule, this letter details infringements and penalties of continued use for the copyright owner's work.
8. Your other option is to research the copyright laws of the country in which the Web page was created and abide by them.
9. Plagiarism is "intentionally taking the . . . property of another without attribution and passing it off as one's own, having failed to add anything of value to the copied material and having reaped from its use an unearned benefit. . . . plagiarism (presenting another's work as one's own) . . ." (Buranen and Roy, 1999, 7).

REFERENCES

Besenjak, Cheryl. 1997. *Copyright Plain and Simple.* Franklin Lakes, NJ: Career Press.

Bettig, Ronald V. 1996. *Copyrighting Culture: The Political Economy of Intellectual Property*. Boulder, CO: Westview.

Buranen, Lise and Alice M. Roy, eds. 1999. *Perspectives on Plagiarism and Intellectual Property in a Postmodern World*. Albany: State University of New York Press.

CNET News. 2002. "Judge: File-Swapping Tools Are Legal." San Francisco (April). Available: http://news.com.com/2100-1027-998363.html (accessed June 7, 2004).

————. "Why File Swapping Tide Is Turning." San Francisco (September). Available: http://news.com.com/2008-1082-5078418.html (accessed June 7, 2004).

Delio, Michelle. 2002. "Deep Links Return to Surface." San Francisco: Wired News. (April). Available: www.wired.com/news/politics/0,1283,51887,00.html (accessed June 7, 2004).

Dorr, David L., Kaye L. Gray, and Terry L. Holcomb. 2002. "Deep Linking: Revisiting and Updating." *TechTrends* 46, no. 4 (July/August): 3–7.

Electronic Frontier Foundation. 2003. "How Not to Get Sued by the RIAA for File-Sharing (And Other Ideas to Avoid Being Treated Like a Criminal)" San Francisco. (October). Available: www.eff.org/IP/P2P/howto-notgetsued.php (accessed June 7, 2004).

Evans, Stephen. 2003. "Tough Lessons for Campus Pirates" United Kingdom: BBC News. (September). Available: http://news.bbc.co.uk/2/hi/business/3201399.stm (accessed June 8, 2004).

Hoffmann, Gretchen McCord. 2001. *Copyright in Cyberspace: Questions and Answers for Librarians*. New York: Neal-Schuman.

Howie, Margaret-Ann F. 1997. *Copyright Issues in Schools*. Horsham, PA: LRP.

Lambert, Pam, et al. 2003. "Facing the Music." *People* 60, no. 13 (September 29): 71–72.

National Association of College Stores (NACS). 2003. "The RIAA and Copyright." Oberlin, OH: NACS. (September). Available: www.nacs.org/public/research/marketwatch/129.asp?id=cmb (accessed June 7, 2004).

"RDTechnology." 2003. *Reader's Digest* 163, no. 978 (October): 218.

Ricciuti, Mike. 1997. "MS Link Irks Ticketmaster." CNET News.com. (April). Available: http://news.com.com/2100-1023-279295.html?legacy=cnet (accessed June 7, 2004).

Ruse, Grosse. 2000. "Copyright Aspects of Hyperlinking." Available: www.eclip.org/workshop/2nd/Grosse_Ruse_handout.pdf (accessed June 7, 2004).

Simpson, Carol. 2001. *Copyright for Schools: A Practical Guide*, 3rd ed. Worthington, OH: Linworth.

Templeton, Brad. n.d. "Linking Rights." Available: www.templetons.com/brad/linkright.html (accessed June 7, 2004).

Torrans, Lee Ann. 2003. *Law for K-12 Libraries and Librarians.* Westport, CT: Libraries Unlimited.

U.S. Copyright Law. 1976. Public Law 94-553, sec. 101, 201.

U.S. Supreme Court. 1989. *"Community for Creative Non-Violence v. Reid."* 490 U.S. 730; Docket Number: 88-293. Available: www.oyez.org/oyez/resource/case/1123/ (accessed June 8, 2004).

Yu, Peter K. 2002. "Conflicts of Laws Issues in International Copyright Cases." Atlanta, GA: Dolesco. Available: www.gigalaw.com/articles/2001 /yu-2001-04.htm (accessed June 8, 2004).

Chapter Seven

Videos, DVDs, CDs, and Copyright Law: Can You Use These Works Legally in Your Classroom?

INTRODUCTION

Elementary, middle, and high school teachers sometimes use fiction and nonfiction videos in the classroom—this is a given. Now with the advent of newer technology, such as the DVD, the showing of movies, for entertainment or education, is becoming even more common in schools, whether in an analog (video) or digital (DVD or CD) format. In 2004, it is probably still more likely to obtain the item you would like to show to your class in a video format. However, DVDs are becoming more and more popular.[1]

Below are questions that cover videos, DVDs, CDs, and related copyright issues. Questions with more than one answer are presented in flow chart form. Remember, when you use the flow charts in this chapter, you are trying to find any criterion under which you may borrow a work. Therefore, you need only follow each flow chart until you come to that point where you satisfy one of the criteria. Once you reach that point, there is no need to go any further. Additionally, for more information on each area discussed, please refer to the chapter (chapters 1 through 5) in which that particular subject is covered.

FAIR USE

Question: You discover that the sex-education video that you always use to support the unit on sexuality in your introductory health class is falling apart. You ask the library media specialist if she will burn it to a CD along with two other deteriorating sex-education tapes that you use all the time. That way you will have the three easily available when you need them, in a format that should not wear out easily, and the original videos can be stored as back-up. She suggests that it would be better for you or her to purchase them on CD, if available, or in video, their old format. You feel that such a purchase would be wasted money. What should be done here?

Answer: Use the flow chart in Figure 7-1 to decide if you should burn a CD or purchase new copies of the videos. It is important to note here, that if you find that you are allowed to copy the videos to CDs that you only show them to your class in the school library. Section 108 of the 1976 Copyright Act, and later expanded upon for digital works in section 404 of the Digital Millennium Copyright Act (DMCA) of 1998, permits libraries and archives to make up to three copies (including digital) of unique or deteriorating works, provided the newly digitized copies are only used on the library or archive premises (Crews, 2000; DMCA, 1998).[2]

Question: Is a teacher allowed to copy a bunch of video clips, string them together onto one tape, and use it in class?

Answer: Use the flow chart in Figure 7-2 to decide if you are allowed to make the tape.

Question: May I show a clip from *October Sky* in my physics class?

Answer: Unless the clip is the heart of the work (see chapter 2), showing it should fit under the fair use factors.

PUBLIC DOMAIN

Question: How do I find out if a movie is in the public domain?[3]

Answer: Follow the steps in the flow chart in Figure 7-3.

DOCUMENTATION AND LICENSES

Question: May I rent an entertainment video or DVD from a video store and use it in my class?

Answer: Section 110(1) of the copyright law states that it is not an infringement for instructors or students to use videos (including those labeled "for home use only") in the classroom, as long as they are using legally obtained videos, and the use is for face-to-face in-

Figure 7–1
Burning Videos to CD

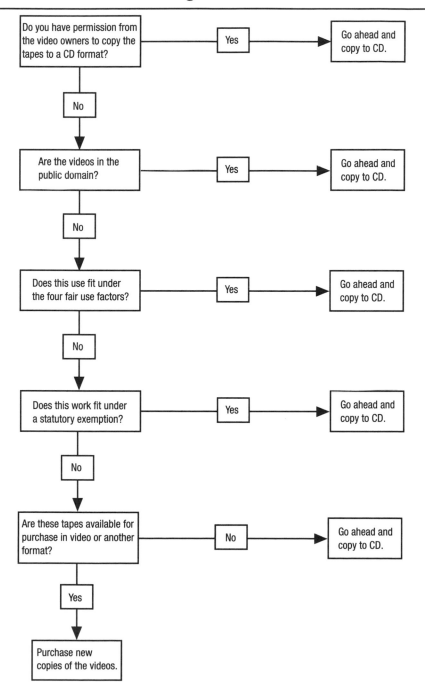

Figure 7–2
Copying Video Clips

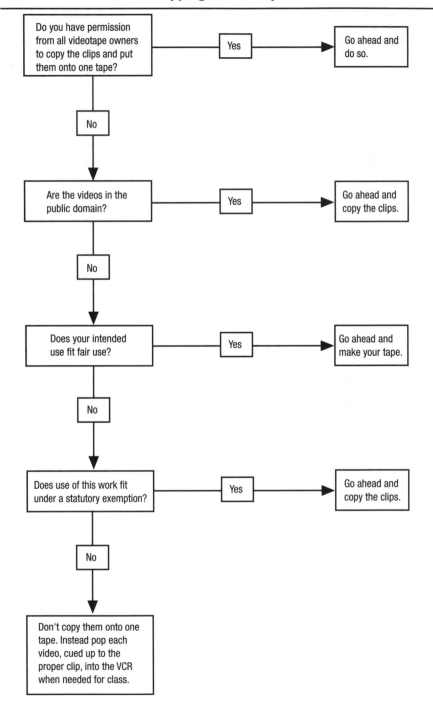

Figure 7–3
Public Domain Movies

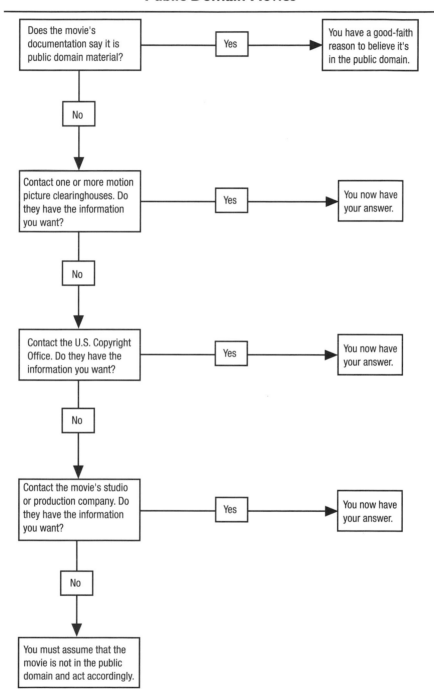

Figure 7–4
Using Entertainment Videos and DVDs in Class

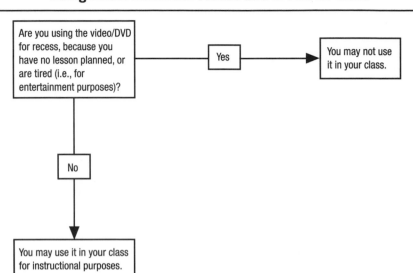

struction in a nonprofit educational institution (U.S. Copyright Law, 1976). Use the flow chart in Figure 7-4 to decide when you can show a video to your class.

Question: The elementary school art teacher paints Disney characters on the lunchroom walls. The kids love it, and ask for more. Is this an infringement?

Answer: Yes, unless you have purchased a license from a company to use their works or otherwise have permission, such use is an infringement of copyright law.

Question: The parent–teacher organization in my children's school is having a "movie" night in the learning center, showing *Where the Red Fern Grows*. They are charging $3.00 per person, proceeds to go towards purchasing more learning-center materials. They tell me that they have purchased "public performance rights," so it is okay. What are public performance rights?

Answer: When a user purchases public performance rights, they have purchased the rights to display the work in a public forum. Public performance rights for a movie might be purchased from a vendor, a clearinghouse, or the owner/creator of the work. (See also chapter 4.)

Question: The eighth grade in my middle school has won recognition for volunteer work in our community. I would like to reward them with a movie in the school auditorium on Friday afternoon. Can I legally do this?

Answer: Use the flow chart in Figure 7-5 to decide if your showing the video is legal. You may find that you have to purchase performance rights. There are also companies that specialize in acquiring permissions from motion picture studios. These companies then sell the school or school district a license to use all or some (usually listed) of the movies produced by each studio. One example of this type of company is Movie Licensing USA. This organization offers licenses for such studios as Walt Disney, Columbia, DreamWorks, Warner Brothers, and others (Movie Licensing USA, 2003).

PERMISSIONS

Question: As the new algebra teacher at the high school, you conceive the idea of having your freshman students create a Web site dealing with basic algebraic equations. To catch the viewer's eye, you want to add clips from popular movies that have a math or numerical theme. How do you obtain clearance to use videos and DVDs on school Web sites?

Answer: Use the flow chart in Figure 7-6 to decide which clips— if any—you can use legally.

Question: Am I allowed to show a DVD over a closed-circuit system to the whole school?

Answer: This is similar to the question about showing a video. Use the flow chart in Figure 7-7 to decide.

YOU CREATE IT, YOU OWN IT

Question: Pretend that you are a middle school technology teacher. You have just finished a unit on copyright law, so your students are focused on borrowing legally. You assign the students, in groups of four, to make a video. All groups elect to use original materials in their videos. They figure that this way they will own the whole work, and thus no copyright violations will occur. One group chooses to film its video outside city hall in front of a new statue the city purchased a year ago. While the sculpture, an unusual piece by a new

Figure 7–5
Using Movies for Rewards

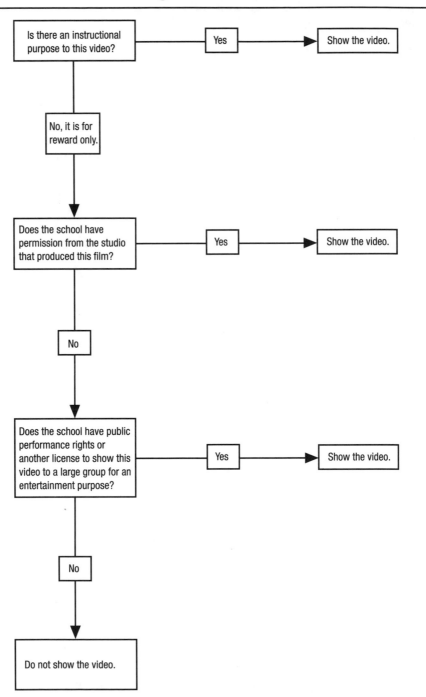

Figure 7–6
Borrowing Movie Clips

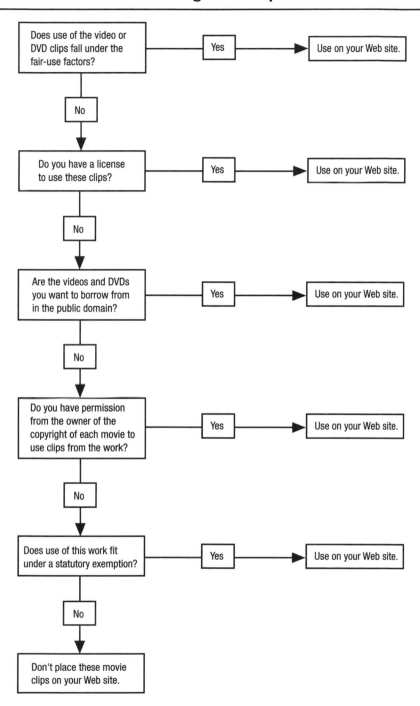

Figure 7–7
Closed-Circuit Systems and DVDs

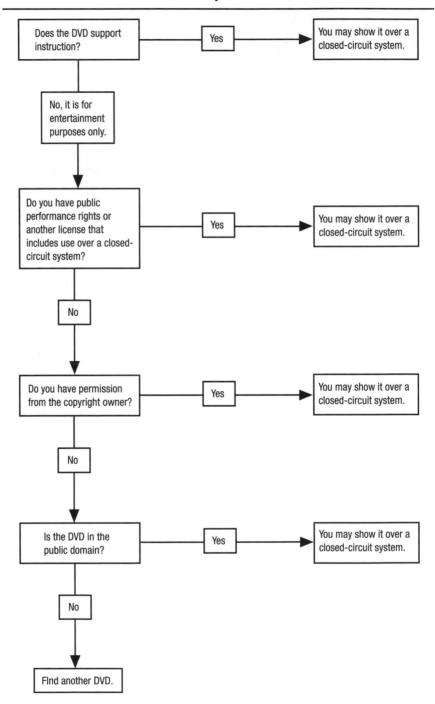

female artist, is very prominently displayed in their video, it is not the subject of the video. Is there a copyright violation here?

Answer: If the artist has chosen to retain her copyright of the sculpture, even though she sold the sculpture to the city, it is possible there is a violation here, since, "It is a fundamental of copyright that certain pieces of art, including sculpture, are eligible for copyright protection. . . . Consequently, permission must be obtained from the copyright holder in order to reproduce images of the sculpture" (Copyright Website, 2002).[5] Students often "get away" with copyright violations that occur as part of a school assignment. However, it is best to follow copyright law in all instances. Figure 7-8 shows a flow chart that provides more direction.

Question: Assume that you are an elementary school teacher. You are about to teach a unit on folk and fairy tales, and you decide to have your students put on a program for the rest of the school. The idea is for your students to act out the stories of "Cinderella," "Aladdin," and "The Three Little Pigs" after they have read and interpreted the stories. There will be no written script. You decide that you will videotape this program to show to future classes, and you want to intersperse your students' story interpretations with excerpts from commercial movies of "Cinderella," "Aladdin," and "The Three Little Pigs." Is it a copyright infringement to read and interpret the original stories on a video? To use the commercial excerpts?

Answer: Classical stories and characters, including the three discussed above, are in the public domain and are frequently borrowed by motion picture companies,[6] book publishers, musicians, and others. So, no, it is not an infringement to tape your students' interpretations of public-domain folk and fairy tales. However, derivative pieces of public-domain works can once again attain copyright when the borrower puts his or her own "stamp" on those revised parts of the work. For example, when an illustrator chooses to draw Snow White as an African-American and the seven dwarfs as Asian, this "new" interpretation of an old work places this interpretation under copyright protection for the illustrator or owner of the work. Thus, make sure that the excerpts of commercial movies you borrow are fair use, under public domain, or that you have the needed permissions. The flow chart in Figure 7-9 will help you decide if you can legally add excerpts from commercial movies to a class video.

Figure 7–8
Statues, Videos, and Copyright

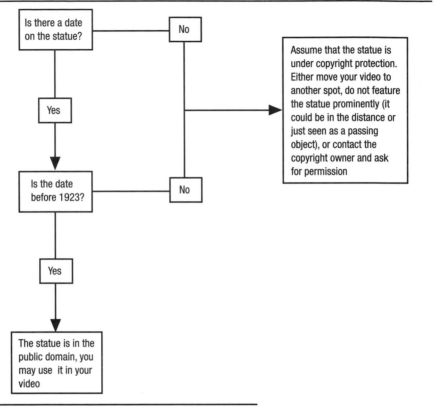

INFRINGEMENTS AND PENALTIES

Question: It is recess time, and it's five degrees below zero out. You make the decision to keep your third-grade class indoors. However, your students need something to do, and you are exhausted. One of your students has brought his favorite DVD to school. Would it be a copyright infringement if you were to show it to your class?

Answer: Use the flow chart in Figure 7-10 to guide your decision.

Question: Pretend that your biology class is studying bird beaks. You find a great video on birding in South America, which you check out from the public library. Can you use it in class without violating copyright law?

Answer: Yes, you can use this video in class without its being considered a copyright infringement. This is because you are using the video since it is for an instructional purpose.

Figure 7–9
Adding Film Excerpts to Class-Created Videos

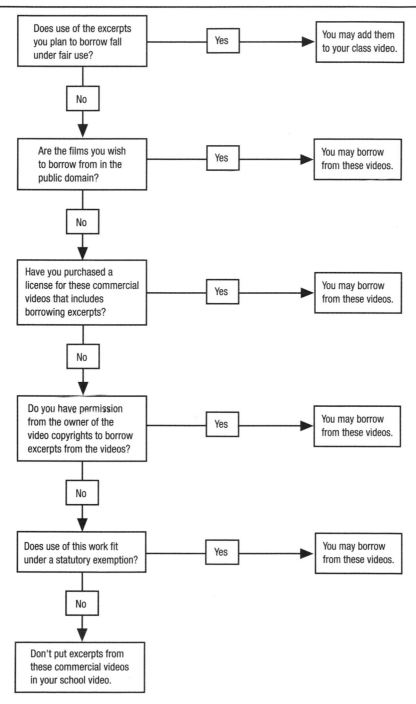

Figure 7–10
Showing Student-Owned Works during Recess

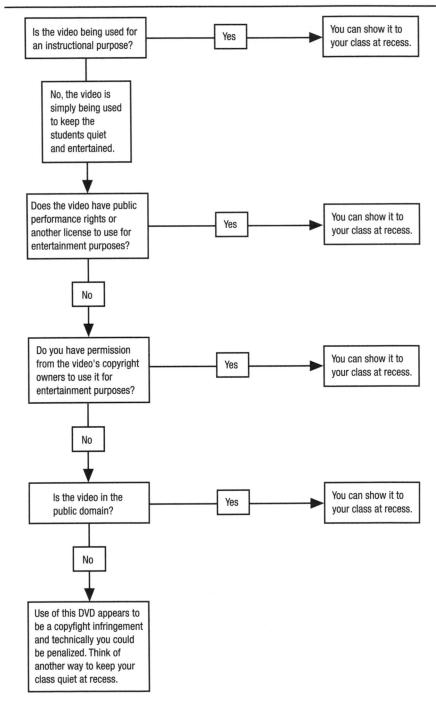

Is the video being used for an instructional purpose? → Yes → You can show it to your class at recess.

No, the video is simply being used to keep the students quiet and entertained.

Does the video have public performance rights or another license to use for entertainment purposes? → Yes → You can show it to your class at recess.

No

Do you have permission from the video's copyright owners to use it for entertainment purposes? → Yes → You can show it to your class at recess.

No

Is the video in the public domain? → Yes → You can show it to your class at recess.

No

Use of this DVD appears to be a copyfight infringement and technically you could be penalized. Think of another way to keep your class quiet at recess.

Question: Suppose you teach science in a very conservative area. You know of a great movie that supports your unit on planets. However, you are afraid to purchase it because it talks about evolution (of the planets), and any mention of evolution is anathema in your rdistrict. You decide to pursue obtaining it from a company that re-edits films, taking out "objectionable" parts. They have agreed to change the term "evolution" to "growth." Your administrator refuses to fund your purchase, stating that the re-editing company is in violation of copyright law. Is it?

Answer: Companies such as CleanFlicks and Family Safe Media purchase videos and DVDs with "objectionable" pieces, edit the media to remove offensive material, and re-sell the derivations to the public.[7] While groups such as the Directors Guild of America and the Motion Picture Association of America feel that this is in violation of copyright law and have threatened lawsuits, currently such editing of purchased materials is not deemed an infringement or subject to penalty (Miller, Campbell, Bane, and Benet, 2003; Russell, 2002).

Question: Your administration has, within the last year, obtained (1) several recordable DVD drives and copying software; (2) CD burners for all teachers' computers and half of the lab computers; (3) more VCRs; and (4) more audio-recording devices. The idea behind all this is that with these recording devices, the school will be able to take more material off popular television, movies, CDs, and the Internet, copy them for use in the school, and eventually save money by purchasing less media. At the moment, the focus in your school is on burning films to DVDs. Overall, your administration feels that they will save money. Do such actions infringe on copyrights?

Answer: Yes! While the past few years have seen a flood of hardware and software that can be used for copying on the market (Lortz and Leavitt, 2004; Shriver, 2002), that does not mean that the copies made from such media are legal. Under copyright law, in this case, fair use, public domain, permissions, and licensing of materials still apply. Therefore, do not use the items purchased for your school for illegal copying. It is in violation of copyright law and subject to penalty.

INTERNATIONAL COPYRIGHT LAW

Question: The father of one of your students has just returned home from a business trip to Southeast Asia. While there, he purchased a DVD copy of a movie, one that has recently come out in the theaters in the United States. The DVD's jewel case has no movie photograph on the cover, there is no copyright information anywhere on the case or DVD, and only the name of the movie is on the DVD. Furthermore, your student tells you that the quality of the DVD is not good. To make things more complex, you search the Internet and find the same movie there as well. What's going on?

Answer: Chances are that the DVD and Internet copies of the movie are pirated. Piracy, the unauthorized replication or use of media, is not part of copyright law, but it is often associated with it, since pirated items are frequently found to be in copyright violation.[8] Since the movie is still in the theaters in the U.S., it is highly likely that use of your student's movie would violate United States copyright law. In addition, the U.S. belongs to several international organizations with treaty agreements in the area of copyright (see chapter 5). Depending on who produced the pirated film and where, this means that such pirating could also be in violation of copyright in other countries.[9] Bottom line: don't use the DVD that your student brought to class or the one you found on the Web.

AVOIDING COPYRIGHT PROBLEMS

Question: I am taking 30 sixth-graders to a natural history museum for the day. This is a full-day school-sponsored outing. The ride each way is two hours long. I would like to take some of my personal videos (commercial entertainment videos) along for them to watch on the bus, which has a TV and video player. Can I do so legally?

Answer: Use the flow chart in Figure 7-11 to decide if you can legally show your personal videos on the bus.

Question: I purchased this DVD from a local store—may I use it in class?

Answer: As has been shown repeatedly in this chapter, that depends on *how* you want to use it. See Figure 7-12 for more information.

Question: A teacher has a favorite video that she shows yearly in her class. Her enthusiasm about this video has caused several other

Figure 7–11
Using Personal Videos on a School Outing

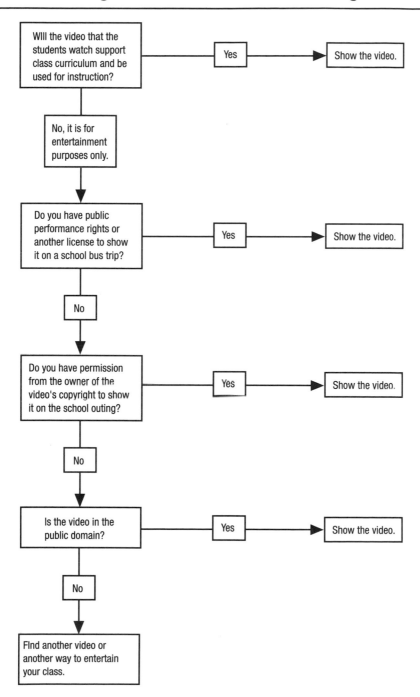

Figure 7–12
Using Locally Purchased DVDs in Class

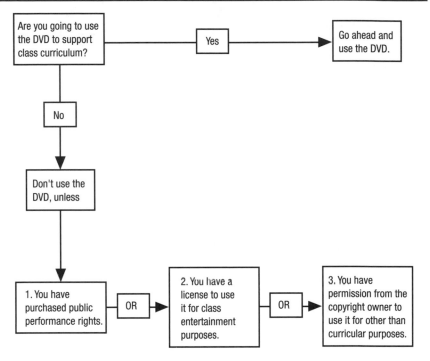

teachers to want to use it also. As a favor to the media specialist, the teacher burns the video to a CD. She then donates the CD to the media center. Is there a copyright problem here?[10]

Answer: Yes! She has just created an unauthorized copy. Throw it out!

Question: Your principal informs all teachers in the school that they may not use any videos or DVDs unless they have been purchased by the learning center. You argue that there are many places videos and DVDs can come from and still be used in the school. Who is right?

Answer: You are. As long as the video is being shown for an instructional purpose, you can rent it from a video store, check it out from the public library, borrow it from a student, purchase it from a discount store, or get it from other sources.

CONCLUSION

In the average K-12 school district today, over half of all copyright questions deal with the use of videos (and, to a lesser extent, DVDs and CDs). Because copyright law is so gray, although there are general rules, the critical answers to video/DVD/CD use in the schools is often missing. The questions, answers, and flow charts in this chapter are designed to help you as you use both instructional and entertainment media in your classroom.

END NOTES

1. While there are still some CD versions of movies available as well, they are becoming less common as DVDs take over the market. Questions and answers for videos and DVDs can also be applied to CD versions of movies.
2. The DMCA also permits libraries and archives "to copy a work into a new format if the original format becomes obsolete—that is, the machine or device used to render the work perceptible is no longer manufactured or is no longer reasonably available in the commercial marketplace" (DMCA, 1998, 15).
3. The U.S. Copyright Office does not maintain lists of works in the public domain. However for a fee ($75.00 per hour in 2003), they will search their records to see if the work you are interested in is part of the public domain. You may also search their online records (yourself) for free (U.S. Copyright Office, 2003).
4. Please note, that in the flow chart in Figure 7-5 (as well as in several other flow charts throughout this book) there is more than one way for the borrower to ask for permission to use a work. You can ask the owner of the work directly for permission, contact a clearinghouse, or purchase a license to borrow the work. (The permission questions are in the third and fourth boxes on the left side of Figure 7-5.) If you satisfy the conditions of one of the permission questions, there is no need to follow the flow chart any further.
5. If the sculpture were the subject of the video, it might constitute fair use. See chapter 2 for a discussion of fair use.
6. For example, Walt Disney Studios often borrow from the public domain (Downes, 2002; Walker, 2000).
7. There are also filters available, such as MovieShield and ClearPlay, that can block DVD content as it is viewed (Miller, et al., 2003; Russell, 2002).

8. Film piracy occurs when an individual or group (1) obtains a copy of a movie on disk or tape from someone in the film distribution area before the authorized release date or (2) actually sneaks into a theater and tapes the movie as it is shown. The stolen copy is then brought to a clandestine production area, where it is mass produced on disk or digitally broken into file pieces easy enough to put on the Internet. At that point it is then distributed. Some such organizations pirate for monetary purposes; others (especially those who place such films on the Web) do it because they feel such media should be free for all consumers (Healey, 2004; Munoz and Healey, 2003).

9. Video and DVD piracy cause U.S. motion picture studios to lose approximately three billion dollars per year in potential income. Similar piracy is destroying the Hong Kong film industry (Motion Picture Association, n.d.; Mullen, 1998).

10. Libraries can sometimes make copies of works that are deteriorating, damaged, or missing, if no replacements can be found, or replacements are not at a fair price (Russell, 2003a, 2003b). This exemption can be found in Section 108 of the Copyright Law of the United States.

REFERENCES

Copyright Website. 2002. "Copyright Casebook: Batman Forever—Warner Brothers and Andrew Leicester." 2002. Foster City, CA: Copyright Website LLC. Available: www.benedict.com/Visual/Batman/Batman.aspx (accessed June 8, 2004).

Crews, Kenneth. 2000. *Copyright Essentials for Librarians and Educators.* Chicago: American Library Association.

"The Digital Millennium Copyright Act of 1998 [DMCA]." 1998. U.S. Copyright Office Summary. Washington, DC: U.S. Copyright Office.

Downes, Larry. 2002. "'Free the Mouse' for Creativity's Sake." *USA Today.* October 8: A21.

Healey, Jon. 2004. "Ego, Not Profit, Rules Movie Pirates' World." *Chicago Tribune.* January 10, Business sec.: 3. Available: http://chicagotribune.com/archives (accessed June 7, 2004).

Lortz, John, and Susan Leavitt. 2004. "DVD Copy Cat: The Difference between Fair Use and Breaking the Law." *Smart Computing* 15, no. 2 (February): 37–39.

Miller, Samantha, Carolyn Campbell, Jason Bane, and Lorenzo Benet. 2003. "G-Rated Revolutionary." *People* 59, no. 6 (February 17): 111–112.

Motion Picture Association, n.d. "Anti-Piracy." Hollywood, CA: Motion Picture Association. Available: http://copyright.org/anti-piracy/content.htm (accessed June 7, 2004).

Movie Licensing USA. 2003. "Frequently Asked Questions: About Movie Copyright Compliancy in Non-Teaching Activities in Public Schools." St. Louis, MO: Movie Licensing USA. Available: www.movlic.com/studioschool.html (accessed June 7, 2004).

Mullen, Christine. 1998. "Video Piracy: It's Time to Say NO MORE." Australia: Jackie Chan Fan Club. Available: www.geocities.com/Hollywood/Set/8801/jcnopiracy.html (accessed June 7, 2004).

Munoz, Lorenza, and Jon Healey. 2003. "Studio Waging Uphill Fight against Bootlegging." *Chicago Tribune*. December 7, Arts & Entertainment: 16.

Russell, Carrie. 2002. "Oh! Those R-Rated Movies: Are Libraries Permitted to Show Edited Versions of Popular Films?" *School Library Journal* 48, no. 12 (December): 33.

———. 2003a. "Searching for a Sign: Do Different Types of Copiers Require Their Own Copyright Notices?" *School Library Journal* 49, no. 7 (July): 41.

———. 2003b. "A Tale of Two Formats: Is It Legal to Make DVD Copies of Instructional Videos?" *School Library Journal* 49, no. 4 (April): 45.

Shiver, Jube Jr. 2002. "Hollywood Lobbies for Stricter Copyright Rules." *Chicago Tribune*. April. Business sec.: 1.

U.S. Copyright Law. 1976. Public Law 94-553.

U.S. Copyright Office. 2003. "FAQ Fair Use." Washington, DC: U.S. Copyright Office. (April) Available: www.copyright.gov/help/faq/faq-fairuse.html (accessed June 7, 2004).

Walker, Jesse. 2000. "Copy Catfight: How Intellectual Property Laws Stifle Popular Culture." Los Angeles: *Reason Magazine*. (March) Available: http://reason.com/0003/fe.jw.copy.shtml (accessed June 7, 2004).

Chapter Eight

Television and Copyright Law: TV Is Free, Isn't It?

INTRODUCTION

Activities such as making a copy of a show from a cable network for class, stringing together a video of television advertisements for an assignment, or saving and using a copy of a popular television program year after year create the possibility of copyright infringement, whether you realize it or not. Sometimes, administrators become so concerned with television pirating that they request that *no* copies of television programs be used in the classroom. However, there is a way to borrow and not be in infringement under copyright law. How do you recognize legal from illegal use of television programs in our classrooms? The discussion in this chapter will help with this endeavor.

The questions that follow cover television programs, educators, and copyright. Questions with more than one answer are presented in flow chart form. Remember, when you use the flow charts in this chapter, you are trying to find any criterion under which you may borrow a work. Therefore, you need only to follow each flow chart until you come to that point where you satisfy one of the criteria. Once you reach that point, there is no need to go any further. For more information on each area discussed, please refer to the chapter (chapters 1 through 5) in which that particular subject is covered.

FAIR USE

Question: When you tape a television show for curricular use in your school, what rules apply?

Answer: Called "off-air" taping, there are several guidelines that apply to instructional taping of television broadcasts.[1] These are publicly recognized as the "Guidelines for Off-Air Recording of Broadcast Programming for Educational Purposes" (Nolo, 2001). Be aware that these guidelines (below) are only in effect "in the course of relevant teaching activities . . ." (U.S. Congress, 1984).

- During the first 10 days after taping, the programs may be viewed by the class for instruction once and repeated once for reinforcement.
- Off-air taped programs may be retained for 45 days. The last 35 days, the teacher may view the tape for evaluation purposes only.
- Programs may be taped at individual teachers' requests, but not for anticipated requests.
- After 45 days, the tape should be erased.
- Location for performance of the off-air taped program should be either in classrooms or other areas used for instructional purposes; in one building, cluster of buildings or a campus; or in the residences of those students who receive formal home instruction.
- The taped program may not be edited. However, you do not have to use the whole thing in class.
- This is a one-time only opportunity. Teachers may not ask for the same program to be taped more than once.
- Taped program must be used for educational use only.
- In some cases, more than one copy may be made of a tape if it is necessary to meet teachers' needs. In such a case, rules for the extra copies are the same as those for the original.
- All off-air copying must include the copyright notice found on the broadcasted program.
- Ask the copyright holder if you need more rights than those normally assigned to educators. Copyright holders often say "yes" to educational purposes.
- Some channels, such as PBS, give more rights (than those above) to educators. Check with the individual networks for this information (Torrans, 2003).

Question: Last Monday night one of the major networks aired a special on AIDs. You tape it to use in your health class. Before showing it to the students, you delete the commercials from the tape. Can you legally cut the commercials out of a taped network broadcast without obtaining permission from the network?

Answer: No, you cannot. By cutting out the commercials, you have created a derivative work. This does not constitute a fair use (see chapter 2). However, you can show the AIDs special basically as you wish by using the remote to run through each commercial. You may also show a fair-use portion of the tape, which does not include a commercial. In other words, while you may not alter a program, you do not have to use all parts of it.

Question: Let's imagine that you are teaching a high school psychology class. There are several popular daytime talk shows that feature people chatting about their problems. You decide to copy short segments, aired during a single week, from these programs and compile them into one tape for class discussion the following week. Is this legal?

Answer: No. Once again, you have prepared a derivative work. Under copyright law, you may not do this without permission.[2] What you can do—although it is more cumbersome—is tape each segment (assuming each use fits under the fair-use factors) on a different tape. Then pop each taped segment into the VCR as you need it.

Question: Can I just copy the visual track off of a TV program for use with my students?

Answer: No. By taking the sound off the tape, you have created a new work. However, you can overcome this by turning down the sound on the TV when showing the students the program.

PUBLIC DOMAIN

Question: I teach social studies and government at the local high school. I want to show my government class the U.S. House of Representatives in action. Can I tape a portion of the House activities off C-SPAN for this class?

Answer: Yes. Floor proceedings for both the House and Senate are in the public domain (National Cable Satellite, 2004a).

Question: Martin Luther King Jr.'s birthday is coming. I'd like to

Figure 8–1
Taping off a Major Network

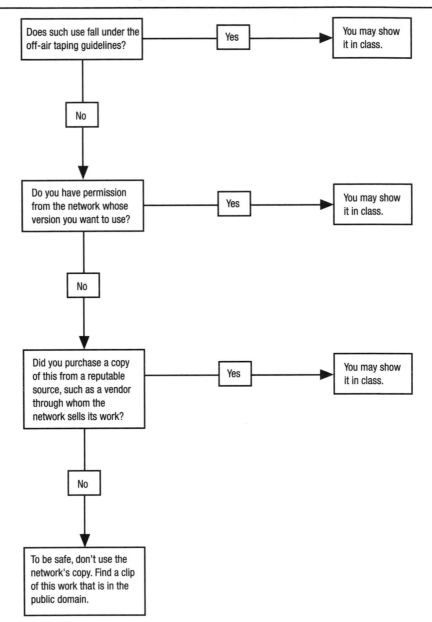

show my students his "I Have a Dream" speech. One of the major networks has a version. May I use it?

Answer: Use the flow chart in Figure 8-1 to decide if you can show the speech you have taped from network television.

DOCUMENTATION AND LICENSES

Question: You are teaching high school history, and you have found a great special about World War II European battlefields on a cable channel. Are you allowed to use it in your class?

Answer: You may be allowed to. The flow chart in Figure 8-2 will help you decide. Some cable networks automatically provide educational rights for a year or more. For example, A&E and the History Channel grant two-year copyright clearances on their Cable in the Classroom programs: *A&E Classroom* and *History Channel Classroom*. Cable in the Classroom episodes of Nickelodeon's *Nick News* have 10-year clearances. Court TV's *Choices & Consequences*, ESPN2's *SportsFigures*, and the Weather Channel's *The Weather Classroom* are copyright cleared for use by educators in perpetuity (Cable in the Classroom, 2003, 1). Also some cable programs grant teachers rights for taping off television that exceed fair use (Cable in the Classroom, 2003).

Many cable networks post copyright guidelines and taping rights on the Internet. It is in your favor to search the Web, before taping, for such procedures. In addition, some stations allow taping for classroom use with some restrictions, for example, the tape may not be taken home by a student, the program may not be shown in anything but a classroom setting, and similar stipulations (Poudre School District, n.d.).

Question: May I use programs taped off C-SPAN in my classes?

Answer: Yes, you may. Here is C-SPAN's policy:

> C-SPAN (Cable Satellite Public Affairs Network) hereby grants educators associated with degree-granting educational institutions this license containing the right to tape any C-SPAN-produced program without receiving prior permission from the network, so long as the copying is for in-classroom use and not for sale, distribution, or any political purpose. . . . The terms of this license constitute a liberal copyright policy that allows educators to record C-SPAN-produced programs (at school or at home) for later use. Such programs may be

Figure 8–2
Using Taped Cable Programs in the Classroom

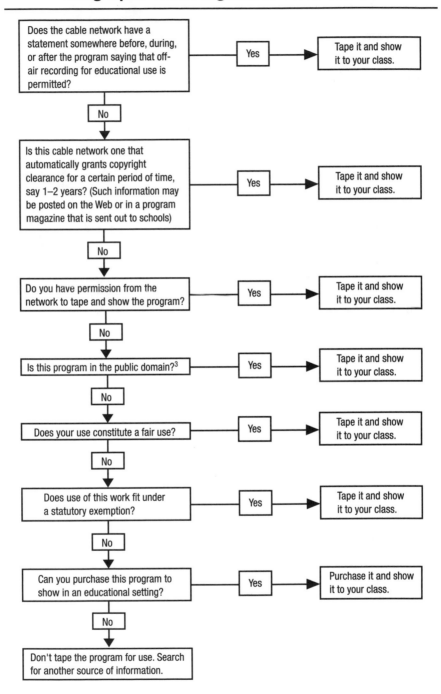

retained in perpetuity for future in-classroom use (National Cable Satellite, 2004a).

In addition, C-SPAN does not charge a license fee as long as the educator follows the terms of the license. Using C-SPAN is a simple way to copy off television.[4]

PERMISSIONS

Question: Is it okay to tape a television program for instructional use in my classroom?

Answer: The answer varies with the source of the program. Use the flow chart in Figure 8-3 to determine what you may do.

Question: I'm a school librarian. May I make more than one copy of an off-air recording if two or more of my teachers need it at the same time?

Answer: Yes. Just follow the "Guidelines for Off-Air Recording." Remember that you cannot add these to the library's permanent collection, unless they are copies of news programs (Bruwelheide, 1996, 48).

Question: The school has a satellite dish. Since the administration pays for this piece of equipment and the television access it provides, the physical science teacher feels that taping programs off it should be free. Are teachers allowed to copy programs off-air from satellite transmissions?

Answer: Satellite and cable have equivalent copyright limitations. See the flow chart in Figure 8-4.

YOU CREATE IT, YOU OWN IT

Question: Several students in the video-production class have prepared short videos about their school, with student and teacher interviews and shots of the school, inside and out. As the video-production teacher, you would like to retain their videos to show as "best examples" to future classes. May you do so?

Answer: If students created their own videos, whether for your class or not, they own copyrights to these videos. As a result, you will need the students' permission to use such videos in future classes.[5]

Figure 8–3
Taping Television Programs for Instructional Use

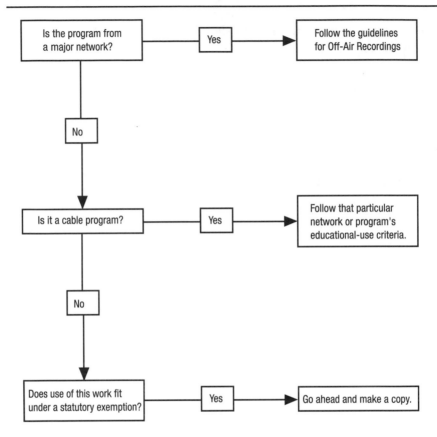

(To this permission request, you might also add how long you plan to use the work and in what capacity. See chapter 4. Reminder: get these permissions in writing and specify each student's name, the particular work, and the class for which the work was originally completed.)

Question: I want to digitize a televised version of *Hamlet,* and put it on our English-class Web site. This way my students can access it at home. Since I have changed the format, may I now do with it as I please?

Answer: That depends on where you obtained the original version of the work. For example, C-SPAN might say "no problem" (National Cable Satellite, 2004b). However, another network might have a digital copyright policy that says otherwise.[6] Given all that,

Figure 8–4
Copying Off-Air from Satellite Transmissions

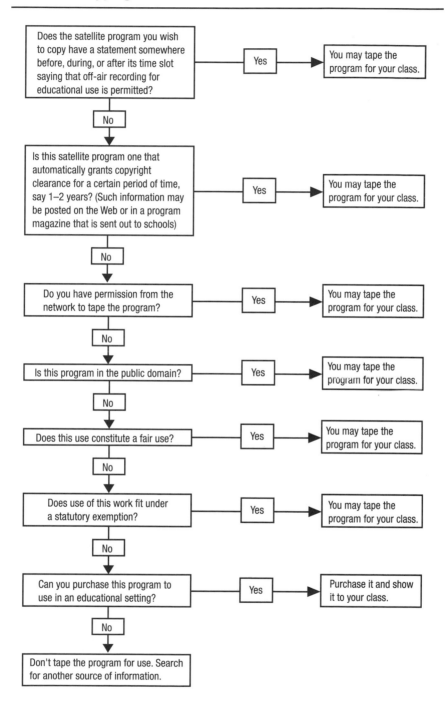

Figure 8-5
Digitizing a Television Program

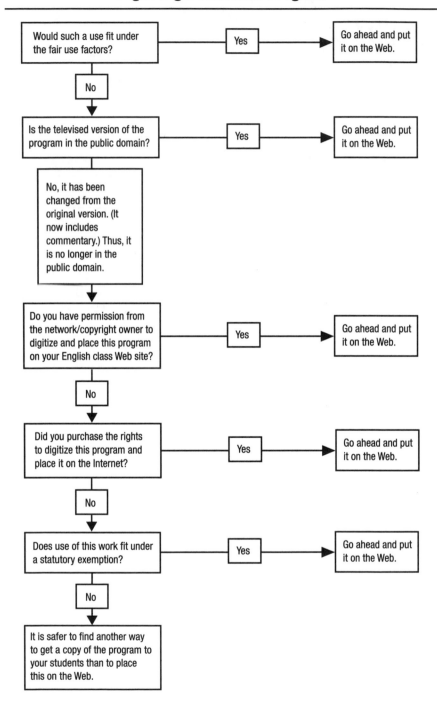

please see the flow chart in Figure 8-5 to decide what digitized television programs you can put on a class Web site.

INFRINGEMENTS AND PENALTIES

Question: I'm an educator, and I'm taping these television shows because our school can't afford to purchase them. I haven't asked for permission, and I know it could be in violation of copyright law, but the kids need this information, and this is the only way I know of to get it to them. Will I get caught? Will I get punished? What would happen to me?

Answer: You may never get caught. Then again, a disgruntled fellow employee, a parent, or anyone else could report your illegal taping to the network. Penalties for illegal television taping vary, from schools' being forced to purchase all illegal tapes, teachers' losing their jobs (or other disciplinary actions), school districts' paying fines, cease-and-desist letters, being required to purchase a license, to adverse publicity for your school community. Yes, you may never get caught, but be aware that there are schools and teachers who do, and they are penalized.

Question: There is no videotape player in my classroom. Therefore, I have asked the school librarian if she will take a program that I videotaped off the television and transfer it to DVD so that I can show it on the DVD player in my classroom. She says that is an infringement of copyright law. Can I get this transferred to a format I can use?

Answer: The flow chart in Figure 8-6 explains the conditions under which transferring a program to another format is allowed.

Question: Your class is discussing how the media influence our culture. To demonstrate this, a student brings a video to school on which he has strung together seven television commercials. Is he in copyright infringement?

Answer: The simplest answer is yes, he has infringed on copyright law since commercials are protected under this law, and he has made copies of them. In addition, by stringing them together, he may have created a derivative work (see discussion above on derivative works). However, since advertisers want people to see what they are selling, chances are that no company will care that he has copied these and is showing them in class.

Figure 8-6
Transferring Television Programs to Another Format

(Assume that showing this television show in its original format is not, itself, a copyright infringement.)

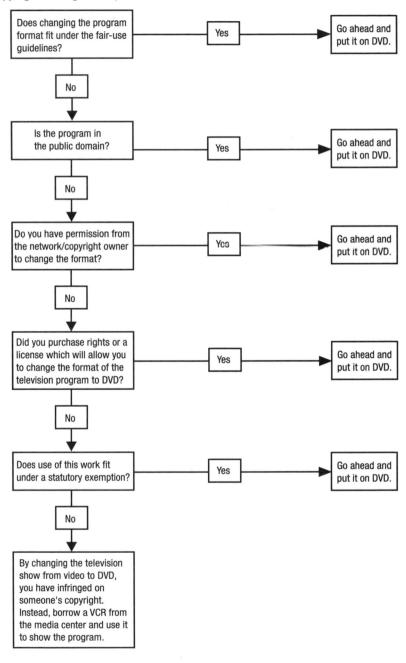

Figure 8-7
Taping Foreign Television

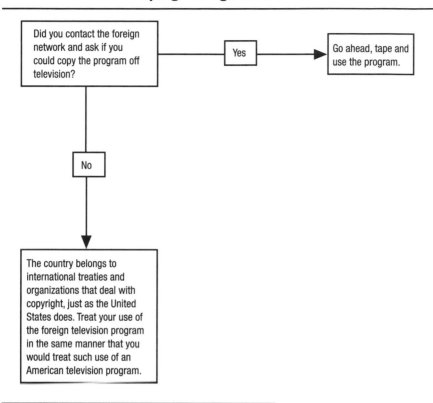

INTERNATIONAL COPYRIGHT LAW

Question: I live near the Canadian border, and we pick up Canadian television stations all the time. Can I tape one of their programs and use it in my classroom?

Answer: Use the flow chart in Figure 8-7 to find out if you can tape a program for class use.

Question: I understand that after 45 days, I may no longer use a television program I have taped. However, it is a great program. I want to use it every semester. Therefore, I plan to ask my grandmother, aunt, best friend, and neighbor to also tape it. I will then use one of their tapes each semester. That way, I can keep using the program for at least four semesters. Is that OK?

Answer: No, it is not OK. Off-air recordings cannot be recorded more than once for use by the same teacher, no matter who records them or how many times the program is broadcast (Bruwelheide, 1995). In this case, it would be best if you purchased the tape from the network.

CONCLUSION

Do you want to use off-air taping from television in your teaching? There are ways to borrow and not be in violation and ways to recognize illegal versus legal use of television programs in our classrooms. This chapter should have answered your questions in this area.

END NOTES

1. Most copyright guidelines are meant to interpret the fair use factors found in the 1976 Copyright Act, sec. 107. One of the ways to access this is through the U.S. Copyright Offices' Web site <www.copyright.gov>.
2. For information on permissions and obtaining licenses for such use, please see chapter 4, "Obtaining Permission," as well as the sections "Documentation and Licenses" and "Permissions" in this chapter.
3. While the network itself cannot be in the public domain, program content can be public domain material.
4. For copyright information regarding digitizing C-SPAN, see National Cable Satellite: "Digital Copyright Policy for Educators" available at < www.c-span.org/classroom/csic_digitalcopyright.sap>.
5. Although the students are the owners of their own works, if the students are minors, it may also be helpful to obtain their parents' permission.
6. According to the *Los Angeles Times*, as quoted in the *Chicago Tribune*, ". . . the Federal Communications Commission . . . ordered consumer-electronics and computer manufacturers to redesign their products to help deter piracy of digital television programs . . . [this] unusual effort by federal regulators to mandate anti-piracy technology to head off potential problems . . . aims to alter digital TV equipment to make it more difficult for programs to be copied on the Internet. The commission said it would not enforce its order until mid-2005 . . ." (FCC Orders Anti-Piracy Measures, 2003).

REFERENCES

Bruwelheide, Janis H. 1995. *The Copyright Primer for Librarians and Educators.* Chicago: American Library Association.

Cable in the Classroom. 2003. "Cable Resources for Education: Copyright and Taping Rights." Washington, DC: Cable in the Classroom. Available: www.ciconline.com/resources/copyright (accessed June 7, 2004).

"FCC Orders Anti-Piracy Measures for Digital TV." 2003. *Chicago Tribune.* November 5, sec. 1: 16.

National Cable Satellite. 2004a. "Copyright Policy for Educators." Washington, DC: National Cable Satellite. Available: www.c-span.org/classroom/csic_copyright.asp (accessed June 7, 2004).

———. 2004b. "Digital Copyright Policy for Educators" Washington, DC: National Cable Satellite. Available: www.c-span.org/classroom/csic_digitalcopyright.asp (accessed June 7, 2004).

Nolo. 2001. "Grading Teachers on Copyright Law—Videotaping for the Classroom." Berkeley, CA: Nolo.com. Available: www.nolo.com/encyclopedia/articles/tc/nn72.html (accessed June 7, 2004).

Poudre School District. 2004. "Channel 10 Copyright FAQ." Fort Collins, CO. Available: www.psd.k12.co.us/services/channel10/faq.aspx (accessed June 7, 2004).

U.S. Congress. 1984 "Guidelines for Off-Air Taping for Educational Purposes." *Congressional Record* (14 October). Washington, DC: United States Congress.

Torrans, Lee Ann. 2003. *Law for K-12 Libraries and Librarians.* Westport, CT: Libraries Unlimited.

Webster, Kathy. 1996. "Copyright Violation Cases." LM_NET. (September 24). Available: www.eduref.org/lm_net/archive/LM.NET-pre1997/1996/Sep-1996/msg01457.html (accessed June 7, 2004).

Chapter Nine

Computer Software and Copyright Law: Why Is Documentation Important?

INTRODUCTION

Unauthorized copying of computer software is against the law. Most of us realize this and can verbalize it readily. However, where do other computer-based technologies, such as works in a digital format, for example, CD-ROMs and e-books—fit in when it comes to copyright? And . . . to expand on the above, what about computer software codes, networks, and CD-drivers—is there a connection to all of these and copyright? The answer is yes, indeed. This chapter will take a look at a number of "computer-based technologies" available to K-12 educators in order to answer questions of copyright law as it applies to various uses. (Please be aware that the term "computer-based technologies" is used here in a very broad sense, to identify a number of things associated with educational technologies that K-12 teachers use and that are in some way associated with computer use.[1] Other computer-based technologies, such as the Internet and multimedia, are addressed in other chapters.)

It is so tempting and so easy to copy—and who will know? The following questions cover a variety of computer-based technologies, educators, and copyright. Questions with more than one answer are presented in flow chart form. Remember, when you use the flow charts in this chapter, you are trying to find any criterion under which you may borrow a work. Therefore, you need only follow each flow chart until you come to that point where you satisfy one of the criteria. Once you reach that point, there is no need to go any further. For more information on each area discussed, refer to the chapter (chapters 1–5) that covers that particular subject.

FAIR USE

Question: May I print off an article from a CD-ROM encyclopedia and copy it for each member of my class?

Answer: Use the flow chart in Figure 9-1 to determine whether to copy an article off a CD-ROM encyclopedia. The "Guidelines for Classroom Copying" (see chapter 5) may also be applied to this question.

Question: May I "borrow" material from a commercially-made computer disk on plant regeneration and put it on a Web page? We are studying this subject in biology, and I want the students to access it from home.

Answer: Use the flow chart in Figure 9-2 to decide if you can put the material on a Web page.

Question: Is computer software code copyrighted?

Answer: Unless the copyright owners say otherwise, it is best to assume that borrowing or cracking computer software code is an infringement of copyright law (Collier, 2000; Sutherland, 2001; Turner, 2001).

PUBLIC DOMAIN

Question: If a piece of computer software that you purchased at a local teacher's store does not have a copyright notice on it, does that mean it is in the public domain?

Answer: No, it does not. It just means that the software's creators did not put a copyright notice on it. Assume it is copyrighted, unless the documentation says otherwise.

Question: Can I assume that educational software I find on the Internet is in the public domain and burn it to a CD?

Answer: No, you cannot. While Internet works are often viewed as if they were in the public domain, in reality they should be treated the same as any other work. If it doesn't state that it is in the public domain, you should presume that it is not.

Figure 9–1
Printing Off a CD-ROM

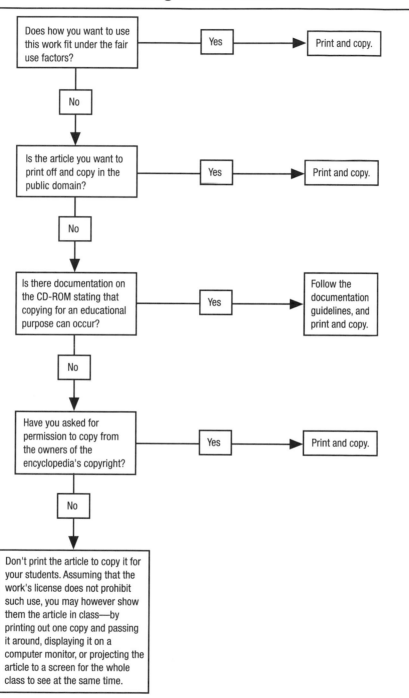

Figure 9–2
Borrowing from Software

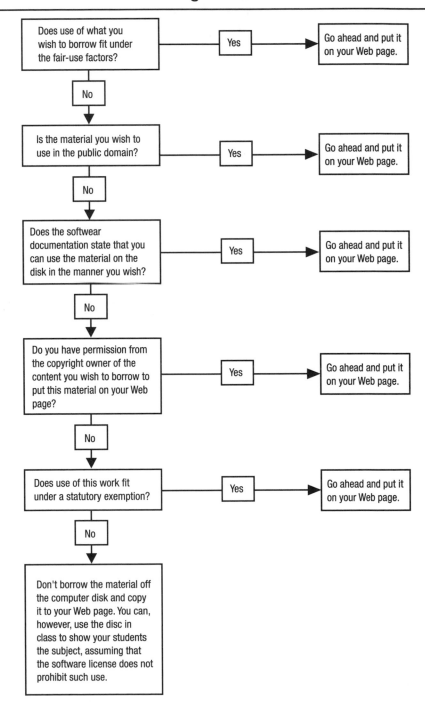

Question: When working in your math classroom, you come across a CD on multiplication and division skills. On the jewel-box lid is a statement from the publisher saying that this CD is in the public domain. How can you use the CD?

Answer: Any way you want! You can make copies to send home with your whole class, print out parts of it for worksheets, use sections on a Web page you are designing. It is yours to use as you would like.

DOCUMENTATION AND LICENSES

When using computer software, it is extremely important to read all documentation first. This is because documentation may include a contract, and contracts supersede copyright law (Singleton, 2002). Reading documentation is a step that many users skip. Their reasoning includes that it takes too long, the words are in too fine a print, it's boring, and so on. What such users often do not recognize is that by not reading the documentation, they may eventually break the law without realizing it. Ignorance is no excuse. If the law has been broken, you are liable. With this in mind, consider the following questions about documentation and computer software.

Question: Can I copy a favorite computer program that I own to my classroom computer for use with students?

Answer: Use the flow chart in Figure 9-3 to determine if you can copy personal software.

Question: Can Mr. Brown's third-graders use the same word-processing program on the 25 machines in the computer lab at the same time?

Answer: The flow chart in Figure 9-4 gives the steps for making this decision.

Question: How can I tell what copyrights the computer software I checked out from the school library media center has?

Answer: The documentation, whether in print format, accessible via the Internet, or on the software, should state whether it is under copyright or in the public domain. In addition, when copyrighted, there is usually a copyright notice on the software. You can also ask your school library media specialist for his or her records regarding this software. The software may have a license by which

Figure 9–3
Copying Personal Software

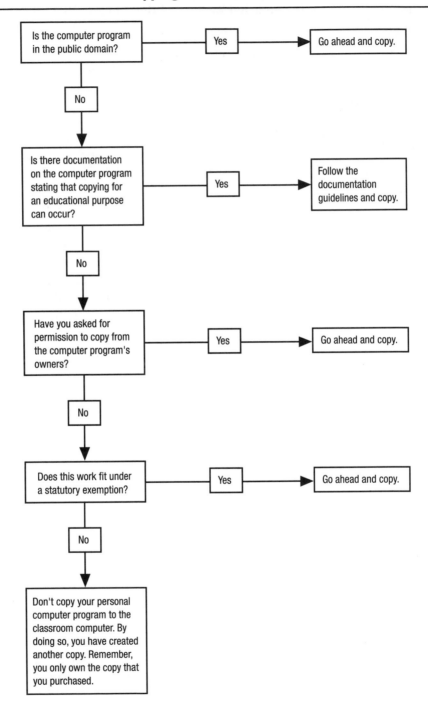

Figure 9–4
Placing Software on Many Computers

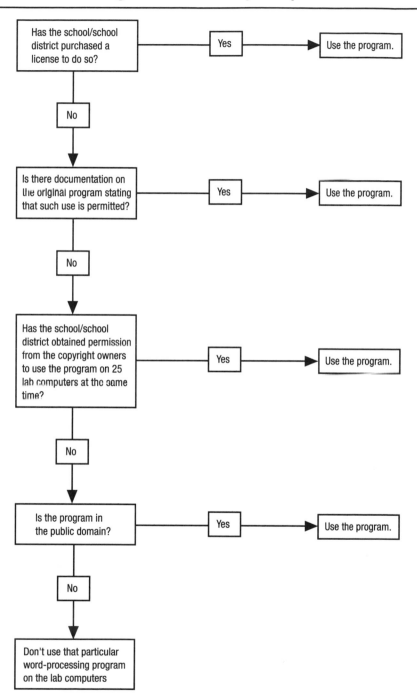

you must abide. It, too, is part of the documentation material. If there is a license, remember that it is a contract and supersedes copyright law. (See chapter 5.)

Question: I just bought a used computer from the school for my home use. There is still a copy of some of the lab software on it. Can I use it?

Answer: That depends on the license or documentation that the school originally purchased with the software. Ask the school for clarification.

Question: Do we treat an electronic book (e-book) like software or as if it were print?

Answer: First of all, protection of copyright is the same for all works, regardless of format. Second, the documentation will tell you how you can use your e-book. For example, the e-book *Dark Shines My Love* by Karen Williams has a copyright statement on page 4 that looks like those found in many books. However, this statement covers many kinds of copying: "No part of this book may be reproduced or transmitted in any form by any means, electronic or mechanical, including photocopying, recording, or by any information and storage retrieval system, without permission in writing from the copyright owner" (Williams, 2000, 4). In the documentation, also look to see if there is any license that accompanies the e-book. If there is, remember that you must abide by that license (see more on licenses in chapter 5), even if what it states is different from copyright law.[2] Bear in mind, however, if there is no license, that all rights and exemptions under the copyright law apply, and that what the copyright owner stated on page 4 of *Dark Shines My Love* is basically a reiteration of some of these terms.

PERMISSIONS

Question: Can I burn a piece of software to CD for safe-keeping purposes? I will then use the copy, and keep the original in a secure place.

Answer: Use the flow chart in Figure 9-5 to decide if this is allowed.

In addition to the above, libraries (including school libraries) may make copies of a number of works for preservation, interlibrary

Figure 9–5
Copying Software to Another Format

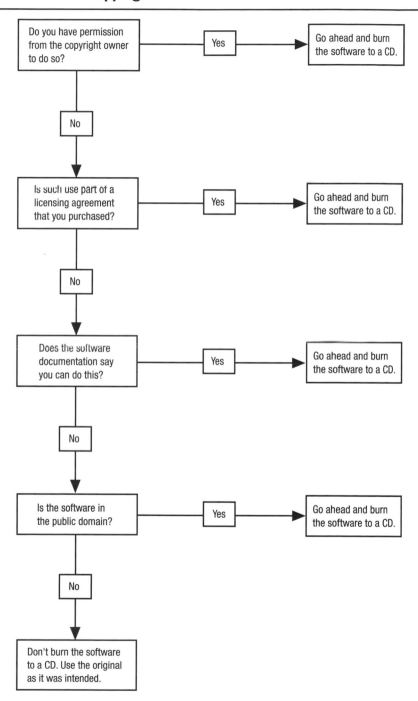

loan, and some private study purposes (Copyright Law, 1976). Let's look at preservation copying. Could it apply to the software in Figure 9-5?

It could apply if:

- the software is deteriorating, damaged, lost, stolen, or in an obsolete format;
- *and* the user is willing to use the CD version *only* on the school library premises;
- *and* the library has already conducted an investigation and discovered that a replacement cannot be obtained at a fair price;
- *then* up to three preservation copies of the software may be made (Copyright Law, 1976; Crews, 2000; DMCA, 1998).

While this gets complicated, it is possible, if the individual is willing to work with the school librarian, that they could find a way to copy the software.

Question: May I send copies of school software home with my students, so that they can get their assignment done?

Answer: Use the flow chart in Figure 9-6 to guide your decision.

Question: My school owns an old version of a software program featuring newspaper templates. We would like to upgrade to a newer version, but we can't find it. Can we just copy the old?

Answer: Assuming that this program really can't be found, under the preservation copying exemption (see discussion above about library copying for preservation purposes) your school library media specialist could make a copy for use in the media center. Before doing this, however, search widely for upgraded software and ask permission from the copyright holder.

YOU CREATE IT, YOU OWN IT

Question: All I want to do is e-mail a quantity of information off some school software to my students. May I do so?

Answer: Use the flow chart in Figure 9-7 to guide your decision.

INFRINGEMENTS AND PENALTIES

Question: A student in your English class brings in a piece of soft-

Figure 9–6
Sending Copies of School Software Home with Students

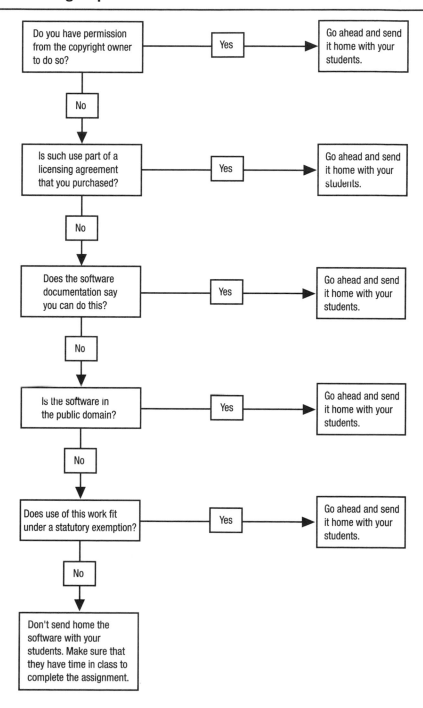

Figure 9–7
E-mailing Software

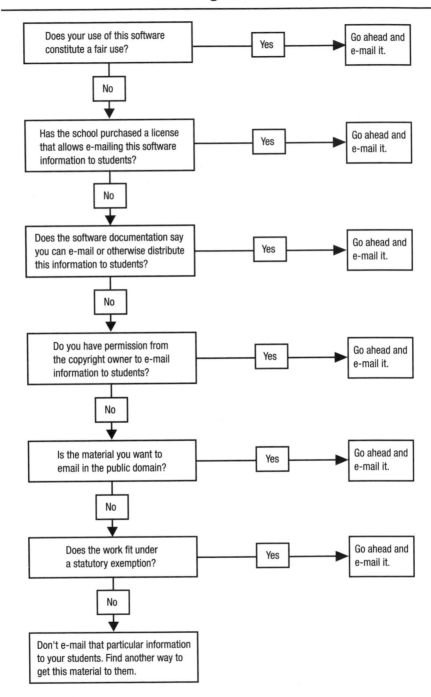

ware that creates footnotes for term papers. He says that it is freeware (software placed by its owner/creator into the public domain). You suspect that it is pirated. How can you tell?

Answer: Illegal copies of software usually have one or more of the following characteristics:

- no documentation is available;
- there are no rebates or guarantees included with the software;
- if the software is labeled, the label looks unprofessional;
- there is no shrink wrap license;
- the disk it is on is a copy;
- the software is already loaded on a used machine you purchased (Butler, 2002b).

Question: Who is liable if a student is caught by a software publisher illegally downloading a program to a school Web site: the student who infringed, the teacher who assigned the unit on which the student was working, the librarian who unwittingly provided the equipment used in the infringement, the technology coordinator who provided the software needed for the infringement, the principal of the school, or the school district superintendent?

Answer: All could be held liable under copyright law. This is because liability follows the "pecking order." There are three categories of copyright infringement. They are listed below, using our example of the student illegally downloading software.

- *Direct Infringement*—This is what the student who knowingly violates the rights of the copyright owner by downloading the software to a school Web site is doing.
- *Contributory or Indirect Infringement*—This is where we find
  o the teacher,
  o the librarian, and
  o the technology coordinator.
     Any or all of these people may have assisted indirectly in the downloading of the software:
  o by providing the hardware or software, and/or
  o by assigning a project that needed that software, etc.
     In addition, these people either knew, or should have known, that they were assisting the student in violating copyright law.
- *Vicarious Infringement*—This is where the principal and the su-

perintendent could fit in, *only if* they, in some way, derive a financial benefit from downloading the software to the Internet. This is because these individuals control, directly or indirectly, the direct and contributory infringers (Simpson, 2001).

Comment: So I've pirated some software. No one will ever know. Besides, they are after the big copier, not "little ol' me."

Answer: Well, that is true. Maybe no one will ever find out that you illegally copied software. (Although, don't forget, that by copying software illegally, you may be violating your professional ethics and modeling undesirable behavior to your students.) Moreover, software producers and copyright owners usually are after those who violate in a big way, copying many programs many times.[3] Be aware, however, that some computer software watchdog organizations and copyright owners offer confidential Internet sites or phone numbers by which infringements may be reported (Software and Information Industry Association, 2002; Business Software Alliance, 2001). No one can guarantee that you will not be caught. If you are planning on copying software illegally, make sure that you haven't made any enemies who might report you!

Question: I don't believe you! Give me an example of a teacher getting caught copying software. What were the penalties?

Answer: In a Chicago suburb, an individual who worked at a school downloaded Acrobat software illegally onto several computers used by school administrators. A lawsuit ensued, brought about by a software group that pursues copyright infringements. The penalties can be extreme. For example, in this case, the school district paid $50,000 to the watchdog organization, the offending employee resigned, and the school district's principals are now required to purchase their own computers and software ("School District Pays," 2001). Penalties vary from case to case depending on the infringements, the court overseeing the lawsuit, those involved in the lawsuit, and so on.

INTERNATIONAL COPYRIGHT LAW

Question: A former student of mine, who is traveling in Hong Kong, has sent me a CD compilation of computer-assisted drafting (CAD) software. It is so much cheaper than buying it in the states! Is it pirated?

Figure 9–8
Pirated Software

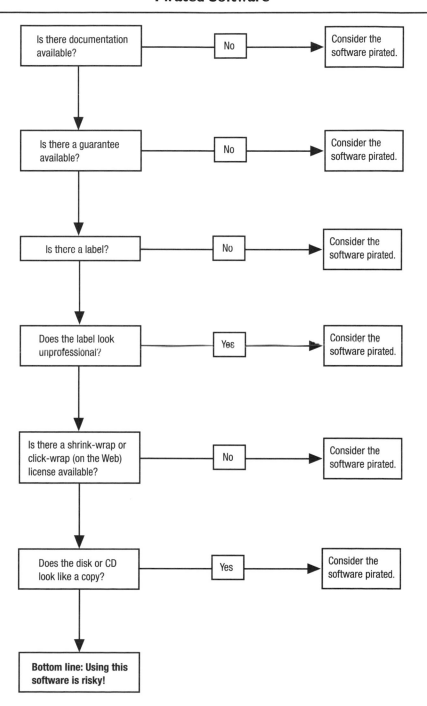

Answer: The flow chart in Figure 9-8 will help you evaluate the situation. In this case, the flow chart steps are not definitive; however, they will guide you in determining whether the software is pirated or not.

Question: Can I use it anyway?

Answer: Since it is so cheap, it is probably pirated. Remember, the U.S. is a signatory to several international copyright treaties (see chapter 5). Your pirated software could easily be in copyright infringement in the country of origin as well as in the United States. Don't use the CAD software that your student sent you.

AVOIDING COPYRIGHT PROBLEMS

Question: Given copyright law, is it legal to install a dinosaur compact disk's CD-driver onto the hard drives of several learning center computers? After all, people can only use it on one computer at a time anyway; that being when the CD is in a specific machine.

Answer: As the technology changes, fewer compact disks need drivers installed to computer hard drives before they can run. Many CDs now run directly from themselves. In addition, as DVDs are developed, fewer CDs are being made. Since the driver comprises information that makes the CD run, it may be protected by copyright. However, there are those older models or those created that still need a driver. Therefore, is it permissible to install a compact disk's CD-driver onto the hard drives of several computers? This particular question can be confusing, because copyright experts disagree on the answer. However, the flow chart in Figure 9-9, while conservative, is helpful.

CONCLUSION

In addition to the previous information in this chapter, here are some steps to make copyright compliance easier:

- Make sure that all documentation is available to the users.
- Consult the documentation—yes, you need to actually read it!
- Ensure that any archival copies of software or other computer-based technologies are kept in a secure place. You may even wish to lock the copies up so that others will not be tempted to borrow them.
- Be sure that your school has a software/computer-based technolo-

Figure 9–9
Installing CD-Drivers onto Computer Hard Drives

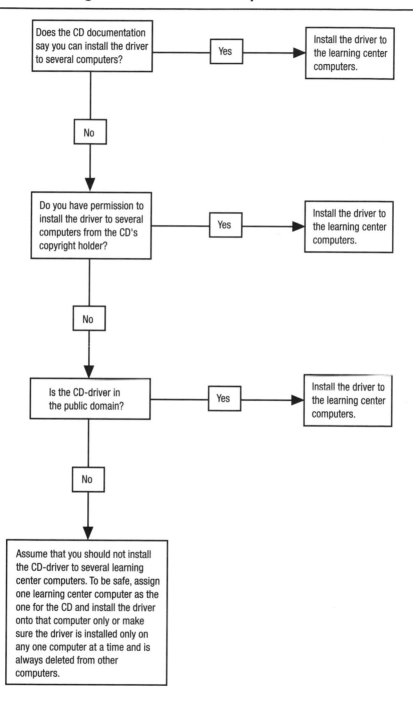

gies' policy and ethics code. If not, encourage your school library media specialist or school administrator to create one and have it accessible to all who use computer software and other computer-based technologies. This code should include a written policy for the use of personal software on school computers, whether in a lab, classroom, or on a teacher's desk. (This code could be included in your school's copyright policy.)

- Be aware of any licenses for the computer-based technologies you use. Some licenses may let your students copy and take home software programs or parts of them for educational purposes. Your school library media specialist or technology coordinator should have a log of these.
- Read all warning notices, such as copyright notices, licensing restrictions, and terms of use—software and other computer-based technologies may contain such notices, for example, during the start-up time. (This may be in addition to the work's documentation.)
- Be diligent in following all documentation and licensing restrictions.
- Understand that not all computer-based technologies' documentation and licenses are the same. For example, some computer software may let you install a copy on your home machine as well as a school machine, while others may not (Butler 2002a).[4]

END NOTES

1. Many of these computer-based technologies are identified and discussed in an article published by the North Central Regional Educational Laboratory titled "Computer-Based Technology and Learning: Evolving Uses and Expectations" (Valdez, et al., 2004).
2. Remember that a license supersedes copyright law (Martin, 2003).
3. A recent exception to the "little ol' me" rule, however, involves lawsuits that the Recording Industry Association of America (RIAA) has been filing against "individual computer users who have been illegally distributing copyrighted music on peer-to-peer networks" (Recording Industry Association of America, 2004).
4. The conclusion to chapter 9 is based largely on an article first published in *Knowledge Quest*: Butler, Rebecca P. 2002. "Computer Software and Copyright Law—Read This First." *Knowledge Quest* 31, no. 1 (September/October): 32–33.

REFERENCES

Business Software Alliance. 2001. "Report Piracy." London: Business Software Alliance. Available: www.bsa.org/uk/report/ (available June 7, 2004).

Butler, Rebecca P. 2002a. "Computer Software and Copyright Law—Read This First." *Knowledge Quest* 31, no. 1 (September/October): 32–33.

———. 2002b. "Software Piracy: Don't Let It Byte You!" *Knowledge Quest* 31, no. 2 (November/December): 41–42.

Collier, Brenda H. 2000. "Protect Your Information: A Copyright Primer for Authors of Computer Software." www.collierlaw.com/articles/swauth.htm (accessed June 7, 2004).

Crews, Kenneth D. 2000. *Copyright Essentials for Librarians and Educators*. Chicago: American Library Association.

Digital Millennium Copyright Act (DMCA). 1998. Public Law 105-304.

Martin, Rebecca. 2003. "The Library: Copyright and Licensing." Classroom handout at Northern Illinois University, DeKalb, IL.

Recording Industry Association of America. 2004. "New Wave of Record Industry Lawsuits Brought against 532 Illegal File Sharers." Washington, DC: Recording Industry Association of America. (January). Available: www.riaa.com/news/newsletter/012104.asp (accessed June 7, 2004).

"School District Pays Copyright Penalty." 2001. *Chicago Tribune*. September 12, sec. 2, 3.

Simpson, Carol. 2001. *Copyright for Schools: A Practical Guide*, 3rd ed. Worthington, OH: Linworth.

Singleton, Solveig. 2002. "Copyright vs. Contract: Shrink Me, Wrap Me, Baby!" Competitive Enterprise Institute. (November). Available: www.cei.org/gencon/016,03292.cfm (accessed June 7, 2004).

Software and Information Industry Association. 2002. "Anti-Piracy." Available: www.siia.net/piracy/report/default.asp (accessed June 7, 2004).

Sutherland, Ed. 2001. "Digital Copyright Controversy Back in Court." NewsFactor Network. (August). Available: www.newsfactor.com/perl/story/12996.html (accessed June 9, 2004).

Turner, Bob. 2001. "Fear: Fight and Flight on the Corporate Battlefield: Should Code Be Protected by the First Amendment?" Darwin. (May). Available: www.ncrel.org/tplan/cbfl/toc.htm (accessed June 9, 2004).

U.S. Copyright Law. 1976. Public Law 94-553, sec. 108.

Valdez, Gilbert, Mary NcNabb, Mary Foertsch, Mary Anderson, Mark

Hawkes, and Lenaya Raack. 2004. "Computer-Based Technology and Learning: Evolving Uses and Expectations." Naperville, IL: North Central Regional Educational Laboratory. Available: www.ncrel.org/tplan/cbtl/toc.htm.

Williams, Karen L. 2000. *Dark Shines My Love*. E-book. Brooklyn, NY: Domhan Books. Available on CD-ROM.

Chapter Ten

Music/Audio and Copyright Law: Who Is Going to Know If You Copy It?

INTRODUCTION

The purpose of this chapter is to cover, in as uncomplicated a manner as possible, information—for K-12 educators—on U.S. copyright law and music/audio in a range of formats. Copyright information for music is extremely complex. Therefore, this chapter attempts to answer some of the more common questions found in school settings, with references to further information, which can be accessed as needed.

First, it is important to define, as does the U.S. Copyright Office, the differences between musical compositions and sound recordings. In "Circular 56a," the U.S. Copyright Office does exactly that. According to their definition, a musical composition consists "of music, including any accompanying words. . . . A musical composition may be in the form of a notated copy (for example, sheet music) or in the form of a phonorecord (for example, cassette tape, LP, or CD) [emphasis added]." The U.S. Copyright Office further defines the creator/author of the musical composition as "generally the composer, and the lyricist, if any" (U.S. Copyright Office, 2003a, 1). "Circular 56a" further defines a sound recording as resulting from: "the fixation of a series of musical, spoken, or other sounds," and the sound recording author as "the performer(s) whose performance is fixed, or the record producer who processes the sounds and fixes them in the final recording, or both"(U.S. Copyright Office, 2003, 1).[1] It may be worded in more "legalese" than we like to read when we are searching quickly for a simple answer to our copyright questions, and it may be more confusing than we would like it to be; however, what is said in "Circular 56a" is that there are two separate kinds of works: musical compositions and sound recordings. They are not the same, they do not necessarily have the same owners or authors (although they can), and their rights under copyright law can be different as well. It is possible, for example, for the score of a musical to be in the public domain, while a CD version of the same musical is registered under copyright. It is also possible that the copyright owner of a recording of country western music that your students want to perform for a parent–teacher organization night is actually *owners*, the performer of the works *and* the recording company who produced the works. With this in mind, who owns what or whom to ask for permission to use the works can sometimes get quite confusing. (This is one of the places where clearinghouses and other organizations that help users obtain the correct permissions for use of works come in. They may save you a lot of time and exasperation! See chapter 4.) You should also be aware, that while the right to *copy* applies to both musical compositions and sound recordings, the right to *perform* only applies to musical compositions.[2] Thus, if you want to perform the song "Evening Mist," unless it is in public domain you need the permission of the owner(s) of its *musical composition*. If you want to copy the sheet music of this song (again, unless it is in public domain), you also need the permission of the owner(s) of the *musical composition*. However, if you want to copy a *version* of this song, which you own on cassette tape, to a Web page, then, assuming the work is not in the public domain, you need permission of the owner(s) of the *sound recording*. Are you still following? Now, let's talk about rights.

Help! Rights to these works vary! While the best way to find out about rights to musical compositions and sound recordings is to study the U.S. Copyright Law of 1976, especially Sections 106, 114, and 115,[3] chances are that this is not feasible for you in the regular school day. However, it is best to be aware that the rights afforded musical compositions and sound recordings under law are not necessarily always the same.[4] Moreover, because confusion abounds in this area, if you have questions that this chapter does not cover or does not cover in the manner that you require, you should consult your school's copyright attorney.

You now know that illegally copying music and other audio is not limited to file sharing (see chapter 6) or transferring music via a boom box from one format to another! The questions that follow cover musical recordings and sheet music, other audio recordings, educators, and copyright. Questions with more than one answer are presented in flow-chart form. Remember, when you use the flow charts in this chapter, you are trying to find any criterion under which you may borrow a work. Therefore, you need only to follow each flow chart until you come to that point where you satisfy one of the criteria. Once you reach that point, there is no need to go any further. For more information on each area discussed, please refer to the chapter (chapters 1 through 5) that covers the particular subject.

FAIR USE

Question: Students in my journalism class are creating Web pages as part of a class assignment. Several want to add audio clips from popular rap songs. How can they do this without it being an infringement of copyright law?

Answer: Use the flow chart in Figure 10-1 to determine what the students can legally do with the rap songs.

Question: I teach students who are blind. As a necessity, all materials I use with them are either oral or in Braille. Can volunteers read books and tape them for my students to use?

Answer: If the selected books cannot be purchased in an audiotape format, then, yes, the books may be read and taped for the blind students to use. Such audiotapes need a notice identifying the original copyright owner and copyright date as well as a notice that the copies will not be reproduced or distributed in another format (Legislative Branch Appropriations, 1997, sec. 121).

Question: I am a vocal music teacher. I like to use popular music CDs and tapes in my classes to demonstrate different vocal arrangements. Sometimes I take songs off several tapes or CDs and either tape them onto one tape or burn them to one CD for class. Am I violating copyright law?

Answer: Use the flow chart in Figure 10-2 to decide if this is a violation of copyright law. There may be exceptions, so be sure to check the U.S. Copyright Office's Web site <www.copyright.gov> for further information.

Question: I am teaching a unit on diet to my third-graders. I want to take a well-known tune from "Sesame Street" and change the words to make a song about healthy eating. This is for a teaching purpose, so there should be no problem with copyright, should there?

Answer: Wrong! You have just created a derivative work, and that is an infringement of copyright law.

Figure 10–1
Adding Popular Music to Web Pages

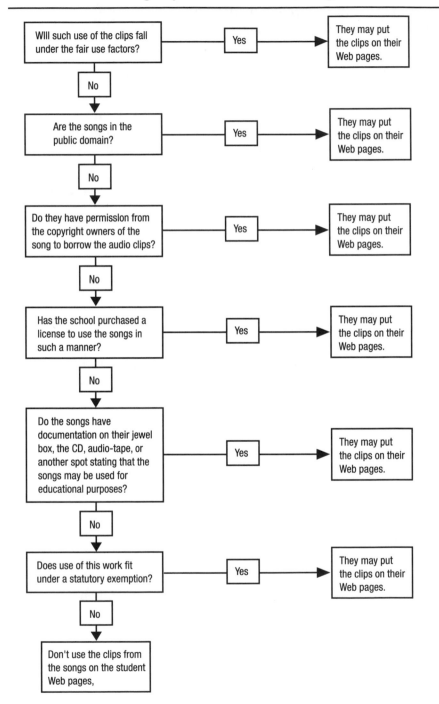

Figure 10–2
Copying Popular Music from One Format to Another

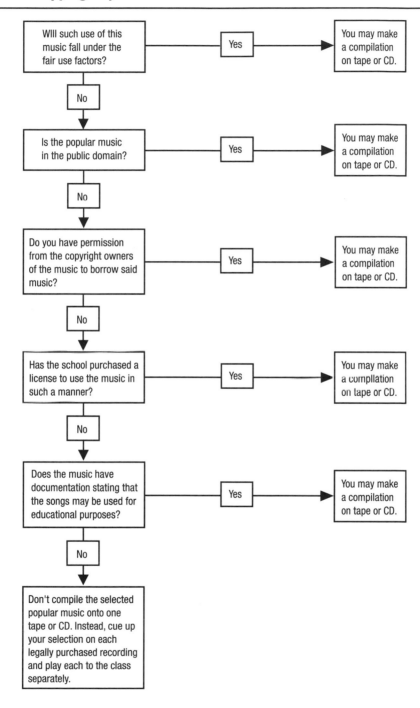

PUBLIC DOMAIN

Question: If I don't register the fight song I wrote for the sports team, is it automatically in the public domain?

Answer: No, it is not in the public domain unless you choose to place it there. Copyright registration is voluntary. Nonetheless, all works become copyrighted the instant they are created. If you wish to file a lawsuit against an infringer, however, it is helpful to have your work officially registered with the U.S. Copyright Office (2003b).

DOCUMENTATION AND LICENSES

Question: The band director is always photocopying sheet music for the marching band. He says that way, he can keep the originals nice, and use the sheet music for many years to come. I say he is violating copyright law. Can he do this?

Answer: Without the proper permissions, he cannot legally copy sheet music for the marching band. Sheet music has been copyright protected since 1831 (Sherman, 2000).[5] Figure 10-3 walks you through the process of deciding when it is permissible to copy sheet music.

Question: When the music department purchases a license to perform a song in public concert, exactly what rights do they purchase?

Answer: The music department purchases the rights that the copyright owner licenses to them (the rights that the copyright owner agrees that the music department can have). These rights vary; they may include the right to charge admission fees for the concert, photocopy the accompanying sheet music, perform the song a specific number of times, videotape the performance, and so on (Christian Copyright Licensing, 2001). It is important that you make sure that you obtain the license or permissions for the specific rights that you need. Fines are often levied to those who infringe on licensing rights (Webster, 1996).

PERMISSIONS

Question: I have a very creative student in my music class. He wants to take a well-known line from a Beatles song and make a new song

Figure 10–3
Copying Sheet Music

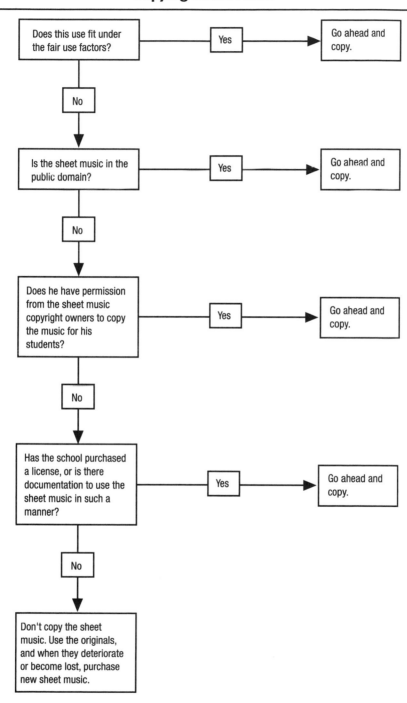

out of it. His idea, then, is to play the song at a school assembly. Does he need any special permissions to do this? After all, what he borrows is such a small piece that it should be fair use.

Answer: First of all, given that this is a well-known line, it may be considered the "heart-of-the-work," which means that, under the fair-use factors, borrowing it would be too much. Next, what your student is doing is called "sampling." It is "the technique of taking a small piece, or 'sample,' of a preexisting piece of music and using the sample to create or enhance a different, new piece of music" (Aczon, 2002, 1). Sampling can violate copyright law for both lyrics and the tune (Aczon; Labate, 2000). Thus, your student needs to obtain permission from the owner of that particular Beatles song before creating his "new" song. Under no circumstances should this "new" song be played in assembly unless permissions for creating and performing the new song were granted to the student.

Question: Is it all right for our cheerleaders to perform routines to popular music at games and other public events?

Answer: In order to be sure that the use of the music your cheerleaders choose for their public performances is not a copyright infringement, your school can purchase a license to use royalty-free music. Such music can be obtained through clearinghouses and similar organizations (see chapter 4) or, more simply, from vendors who deal in such music. These vendors either obtain permissions from copyright owners or find public-domain music. The vendors then put this music into collections, which they sell for a fee to schools and other groups who need public performance music. Often, these royalty-free music vendors have educational prices and sell schools blanket permissions to use the music any way they wish, from public performances to multimedia productions (*Royalty Free Music Library*, 2003). There are other options, as well, for obtaining the use of music for public performances, so check the U.S. Copyright Offices Web site <www.copyright.gov>. For example, the school could contact directly one of the clearinghouses that deals in licenses for popular music performances.[6] See also Figure 10-4 for guidance in making your decisions.

Question: Can my students print off the words to popular songs from an Internet site? They are using the lyrics as poetry examples for my English class.

Answer: Use the flow chart in Figure 10-5 to guide your decision.

Figure 10–4
Performing Popular Music at Public Events

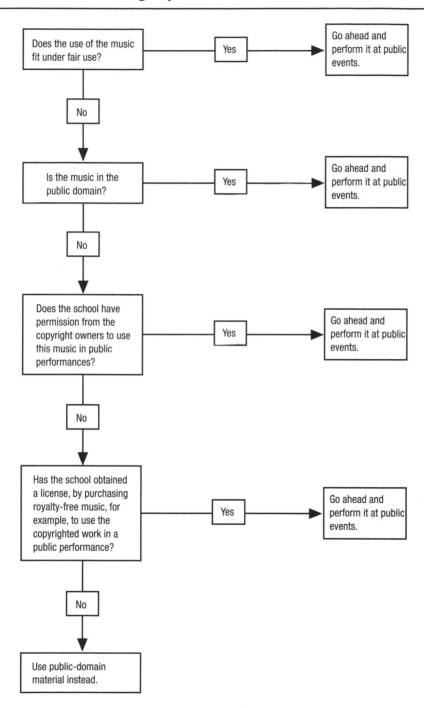

Also check the Web site of the U.S. Copyright Office <www.copyright.gov> for exceptions.

Question: For a school project organized by our principal, several local celebrities, including the mayor and our state senator, read stories to our elementary school classes. These stories were audio-taped and put in the media center for check-out. No attempt was made to discover if there were already audio-taped versions of these stories available for purchase. I am the media specialist, and I am very concerned about this. I think that we may be violating copyright law. Am I right?[7]

Answer: Use the flow chart in Figure 10-6 to decide if this is a violation of copyright. Check the U.S. Copyright Office's site <www.copyright.gov> for exceptions.

You cannot presume that these books can be audio-taped, stored in the media center, and used for circulation purposes, no matter who is reading them or what the project is. Each book must be individually studied to determine whether it can be audio-taped by the volunteers and celebrities.

Question: One of my students wrote and performed an original song for a school holiday concert. She says that her parents told her about something called a "poor man's copyright." Should she use this to copyright her song?

Answer: It is a fallacy that sending a copy of your original work to yourself is a "poor man's copyright" (U.S. Copyright Office, 2003b). The "poor man's copyright" is meaningless under current copyright law because works are protected under copyright from the moment they are created. You can, however, officially register your work with the U.S. Copyright Office (see chapter 1).

INFRINGEMENTS AND PENALTIES

Question: One of my library aides wants to take the song "You're No Good" and create a satirical song about cheese titled "You're No Gouda." Is this an infringement of copyright law?

Answer: No, if the use of the original song fits under the fair-use factors. Although it appears that she has created a derivative work, what she has done is to make fun of the original work. As long as such use fits under fair use, you don't need permission to make a parody.[8]

Figure 10–5
Printing Lyrics off the Internet

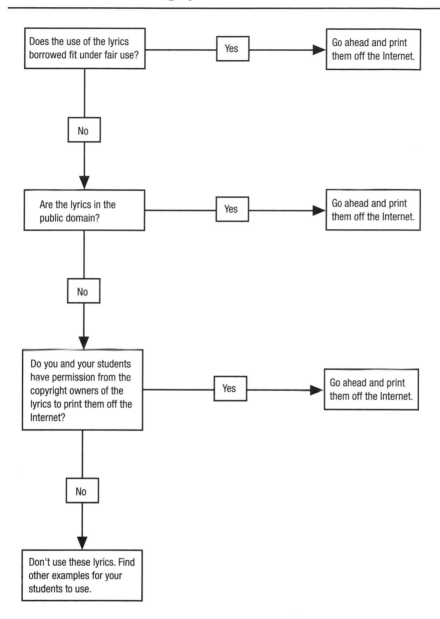

Question: I have asked a technologically-astute student to create a Web page for our class. He wants to borrow music from another site and put it on our site. Is this an infringement of copyright law?

Figure 10–6
Audio-Taping Picture Books

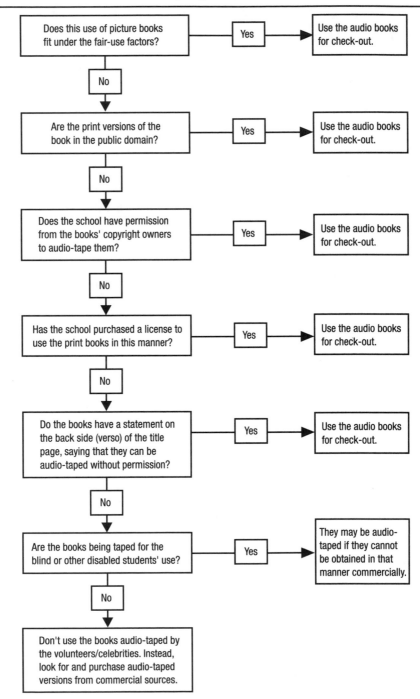

Answer: Use the flow chart in Figure 10-7 to decide if this is an infringement of the law. Also check the U.S. Copyright Office's site <www.copyright.gov> for exceptions.

Always read the documentation on Internet sites. It is possible that a specific site will provide a statement saying that works from that site can be used, with or without acknowledging the original site, on school or other educational Web pages (FA©E, n.d.).

Question: Help! Part of the school sheet music collection was damaged in last night's rain storm. The leak in the roof destroyed all but one piece of the altos' parts. We have a concert tonight. Can we legally copy the altos' part several times for the concert?

Answer: Yes, it can be copied for the concert only. Include the copyright notice, found on the original sheet music, on the copy as well as any appropriate recognition to the sheet music source. Destroy the copies after the concert and purchase more originals, if they are available (Harper, 2001).

INTERNATIONAL COPYRIGHT LAW

Question: For the middle school variety show, you have asked a student to dress up like Elvis, mimic his movements, and mouth the words to one of his songs. The student in question purchased a recording of Elvis' works when he and his family went to Europe last summer, and you notice that the recording has a European copyright on it. Can you use this recording in your variety show?

Answer: Much of Europe belongs to the same international copyright treaties and organizations as the United States. Thus, you should treat the Elvis recording purchased in Europe in the same manner that you would treat one purchased in the United States. See Figure 10-8.

AVOIDING COPYRIGHT PROBLEMS

Question: Can the school library tape multiple copies of a school orchestra concert for distribution in student homes? (They will not charge for doing this.)

Answer: Use the flow chart in Figure 10-9 to decide if the tapes are allowed under copyright law. Consult the U.S. Copyright

Figure 10–7
Borrowing Music from One Web Site for Another

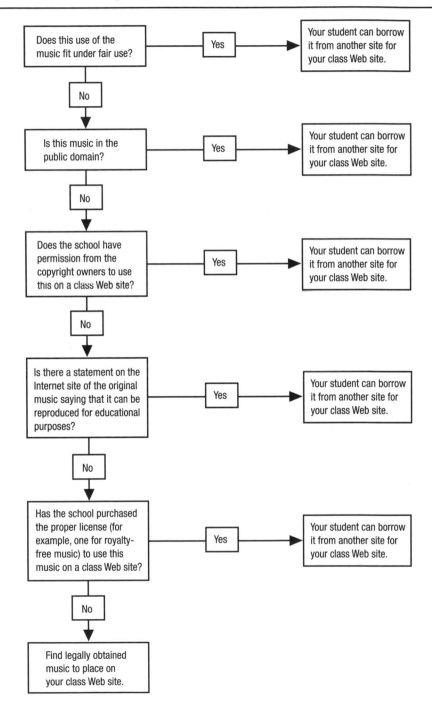

Figure 10–8
Using a Popular Recording for a Public Performance

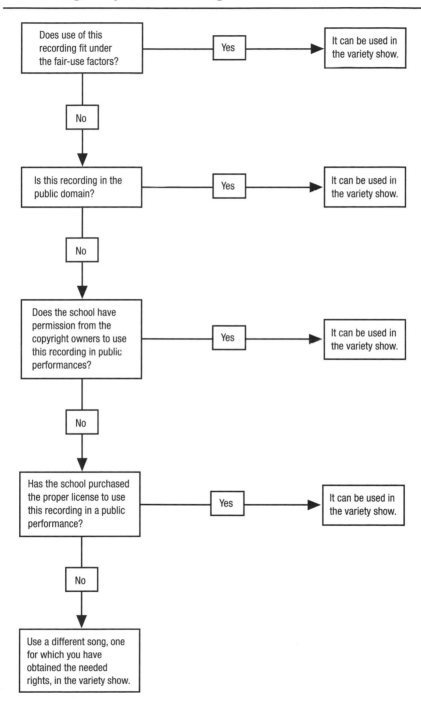

Office's site <www.copyright.gov> for exceptions and further information.

Question: Can a local business record an elementary choral concert, edit it, and sell it to parents and the local community?

Answer: In all probability, such a money-making scheme is a copyright infringement. Yet, there are some instances—however unusual—in which it would be possible for the local business to do this. (See Figure 10-10.)

Question: We charge admission to our high school basketball games. Are we allowed to play popular music at intermission or before the game starts?

Answer: Use the flow chart in Figure 10-11 to determine if the music may be played.

CONCLUSION

When studying audio formats, sheet music, and copyright, the following are important to investigate: fair use, public domain, permissions, documentation, licenses, and royalty-free music companies. All, at one time or another, will help users employ sound materials without copyright infringements.

Figure 10–9
Free-of-Charge Taping of School Concerts for Home Distribution

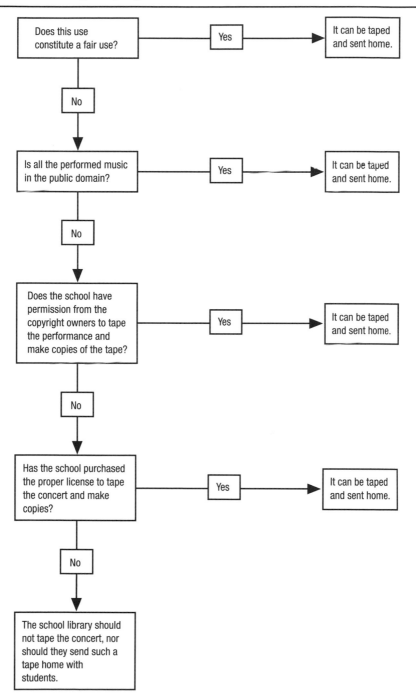

Figure 10–10
For-Profit Taping of School Concerts for Home Distribution

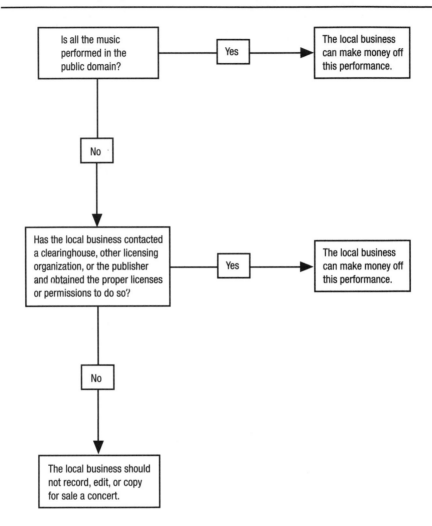

Figure 10–11
Playing Popular Music at School Sporting Events

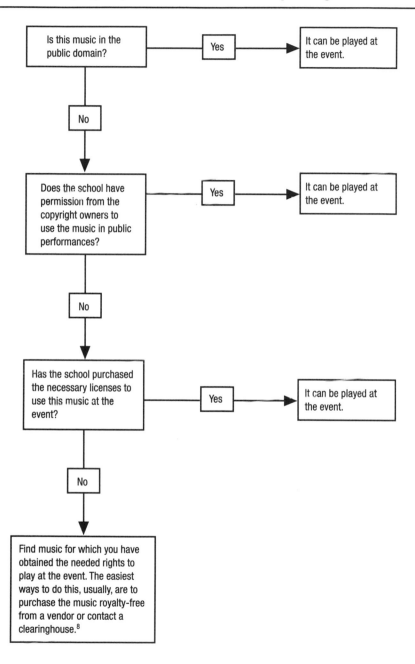

END NOTES

1. Sound recordings do not include the sounds accompanying motion pictures or other audiovisual works (U.S. Copyright Office, 2000).
2. Like most things dealing with copyright, there are exceptions. For more information in this area, go to the U.S. Copyright Office at www.copyright.gov/.
3. Sections 107-121 also have information on the topic.
4. For example, if CDs, cassette tapes, etc. (musical compositions) have been distributed to the public, then a compulsory license is required to duplicate these works. However, for reproductions of sound recordings, no mention is made of a compulsory license; nonetheless, their rights include the right to reproduce the original music or other sounds (Bell, 2002; U.S. Copyright Office, 2004).

   To take a more specific example, suppose you wrote a song. You created the sheet music (notes and lyrics). You also created a CD version in which you sing this song. What you have created is the musical composition. Now, say that you sell the rights to perform your song to Garth Brooks and Sony Records. The CDs, audiotapes, etc., that Garth performs and that Sony Records produces are owned by them—depending on their agreement it may be owned by either one or by both. These are the sound recordings and the owner of the copyright (Garth, Sony, or both) has the right to reproduce the music.

   Web sites to go for helpful information on music/audio copyrights include the U.S. Copyright Office at www.copyright.gov/ and the "Music Copyrights Table" at www.tomwbell.com/teaching/Music(C)s.html.
5. In addition, there are guidelines for the copying of classroom materials and music that might apply, given the right parameters. See chapter 5: "Other Important Copyright Concepts" for more information on this. Also there may be exceptions. See U.S. Copyright Office at <www.copyright.gov> as well.
6. Some of the clearinghouses that represent such groups as songwriters, composers, music publishers, and recording labels are the American Society of Composers, Authors and Publishers (ASCAP), Broadcast Music, Inc. (BMI), the Harry Fox Agency, and the Recording Industry Association of America (RIAA).
7. In addition, there may be other issues to be concerned about when dealing with local celebrities, including politicians, who are reading picture books onto tape. One issue would be the right of pub-

licity. "The Right of Publicity prevents the unauthorized commercial use of an individual's name, likeness, or other recognizable aspects of one's persona. It gives an individual the exclusive right to license the use of their identity for commercial promotion." (Legal Information Institute, 2004, 1) For the purposes of the "audiotaping picture books" question, however, we are going to assume that the local celebrities are volunteering their names and likenesses, as well as their time.

8. Section 107 of the U.S. Copyright law states that "the fair use of a copyrighted work . . . for purposes such as criticism [or] comment . . . is not an infringement. . . ." (U.S. Copyright Law, 1976, sec. 107, 16).

9. While purchasing royalty-free music from a vendor and contacting a clearinghouse both involve spending a little money, it is usually worth it. Both the vendors and the clearinghouses are obtaining consent for you to use the music in specified ways. Essentially, they are obtaining licenses/permissions for you.

REFERENCES

Aczon, Michael A. 2002. "Sampling and Copyright—How to Obtain Permission to Use Samples." Primedia Business Magazines and Media. (March). Available: http://emusician.com/tutorials/emusic_clear/index.html (accessed June 9, 2004).

Bell, Tom, W. 2002. "Music Copyrights Table." Orange, CA: Teaching Materials. Available: www.tomwbell.com/teaching/Music(C)s.html (accessed June 7, 2004).

Christian Copyright Licensing International. 2001. "FAQs." Portland, OR: Christian Copyright Licensing International. Available: www.ccli.com/Visitors/FAQ.cfm (accessed June 7, 2004).

FA©E. n.d. "Friends of Active Copyright Education." Copyright Society of the U.S.A. Available: www.csusa.org/face/index.htm (accessed June 7, 2004).

Harper, Georgia. 2004. "Fair Use of Copyrighted Materials." Austin: University of Texas. (April). Available: www.utsystem.edu/ogc/intellectualproperty/copypol2.htm (accessed June 9, 2004).

Labate, Robert J. 2000. "Setting Up Shop on the Internet." *Performink* (January): 18.

Legal Information Institute. 2004. "Law about . . . Right of Publicity: An Overview." Ithaca, NY: Cornell University Law School. (May). Available: www.law.cornell.edu/topics/publicity.html (accessed June 7, 2004).

Legislative Branch Appropriations Act of 1996. 1997. Public Law No. 104-197, sec. 110, 121.

Royalty Free Music Library. 2003. [Pamphlet.] Atlanta, GA: Soundzabound Music Library.

Russell, Carrie. 2003. "A Get-Rich-Quick Scheme? Your School's Fund-Raiser May Not Qualify for a Copyright Exemption." *School Library Journal* 49, no. 2 (February): 43.

Sherman, Chris. 2000. "Napster: Copyright Killer or Distribution Hero?" *Online* 24, no. 6 (November): 18–28. Available: www.findarticles.com/cf_0/m1388/6_24/66456907/print.jhtml (accessed June 7, 2004).

U.S. Copyright Law. 1976. Public Law 94-553.

U.S. Copyright Office, Library of Congress. 2000. "Form of Notice for Phonorecords of Sound Recordings." Washington, DC: U.S. Copyright Office.

————. 2003a. *"Circular 56a": Copyright Registration of Musical Compositions and Sound Recordings*. Washington, DC: U.S. Copyright Office.

————. 2003b. "Frequently asked Questions About Copyright: Copyright in General." (April). Available: www.copyright.gov/help/faq/faq-general.html (accessed June 7, 2004).

U.S. Copyright Office, Library of Congress. 2004. Available: www.copyright.gov (accessed June 7, 2004).

Webster, Kathy. 1996. "Copyright Violation Cases." LM_NET (September 24). Available: www.eduref.org/lm_net/archive/LM_NET-pre1997/1996/Sep_1996/msg01457.html (accessed June 7, 2004).

Chapter Eleven

Multimedia and Copyright Law: How Confusing! Can You Borrow a Variety of Works for Your Production?

INTRODUCTION

For the purposes of this chapter, multimedia is defined as "A term that is used generically to refer to the many different mediums that computer and Web pages can support all at once, including text, graphics, audio, and video" (Congress Online Project, 2004). Multimedia works are used in both face-to-face and online teaching. Because they may contain a number of separate works, each with its own copyright protection, multimedia is addressed in this book. The questions that follow cover multimedia productions, educators, and copyright law. Questions with more than one answer are presented in flow-chart form. Remember, when you use the flow charts in this chapter, you are trying to find any criterion under which you may borrow a work. Therefore, you need only to follow each flow chart until you come to that point where you satisfy one of the criteria. Once you reach that point, there is no need to go any further. For more information on each area discussed, refer to the chapter (chapters 1 through 5) that covers that particular subject.

FAIR USE

Question: A technology teacher assigns a group project; the project is to make a multimedia production. One group borrows liberally for their multimedia assignment: a song from a music CD, a clip from a video, a cartoon from a newspaper Internet site, a poem from a print anthology, and a graphic from a Web site. Can they borrow these works under copyright law?

Answer: Yes, they can, if the use fits in the flow chart in Figure 11-1.[1] Since this is an assignment, fair use for students can be interpreted as that amount needed to achieve the learning goal; this means that if a whole song is needed to achieve the assignment's goal, then the whole song falls under the fair-use guidelines (Russell, 2003). Remember, the smallest amount you need is the amount you should use. Such multimedia projects should be used for class or student portfolios only.

Question: Is it okay for my students to put photographs in their multimedia project?

Answer: Use the flow chart in Figure 11-2 to determine if the students may use photographs.[2]

Question: When creating multimedia projects, do I have to use the "Fair Use Guidelines for Educational Multimedia?" (American Distance Education Consortium, 2003).

Answer: No. While some educators use the "Fair Use Guidelines for Educational Multimedia" (see chapter 2) to measure how much of protected works can be used in multimedia projects, in this chapter I primarily use the four fair use factors[3] found under Section 107 of the 1976 copyright law (see also chapter 2). I do this because under fair use (U.S. Copyright Law, sec. 107) more can be borrowed than is allowed under the conservative interpretation of the four fair use factors, the "Fair Use Guidelines for Educational Multimedia."[4]

PUBLIC DOMAIN

Question: I found a multimedia work on the Web. There is no copyright notice on it. Therefore, it is in the public domain, and I can use it any way I want, correct?

Answer: No, that is not correct. It just means that the owner/creator did not put a copyright notice on it. Unless the Web site specifically states that the multimedia work is in the public domain, you must assume that it is copyrighted and treat it accordingly.

Figure 11–1
Borrowing a Variety of Works for a Multimedia Production

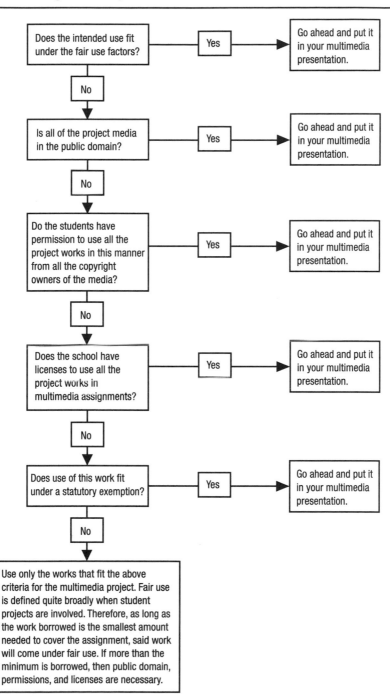

Figure 11–2
Using Photographs in Multimedia Projects

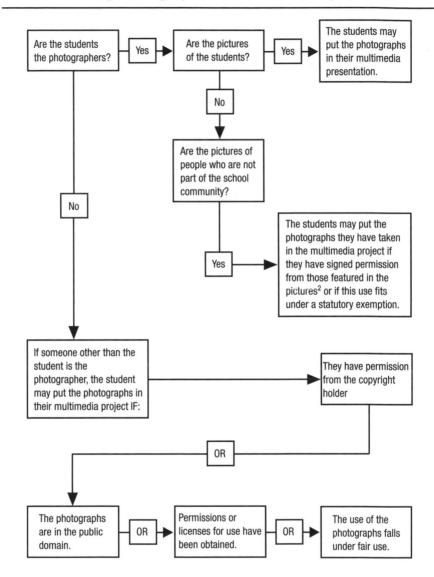

Question: I want to use a song in my multimedia presentation. I have been told that there are a lot of public-domain songs on the Web. When I search, what do I look for in order to find one?

Answer: Other than the words, "public domain," keywords that will help are "original, classical, anonymous, or traditional" (Davis, 1998, 1). It is important to remember here that just because you get a hit on one of the keywords above, it does *not* mean that the songs you find are in the public domain. These terms simply should make such searching easier. Remember that there is no guarantee that a work will be in the public domain.

Question: How do I put my multimedia work into the public domain?

Answer: If you are the owner of your multimedia work, and all contents of the multimedia product also belong to you, it is easy to transfer your rights (U.S. Copyright Office, 2003a). In the case of public domain, you just label your work, "public domain." If you have borrowed some or all of the contents of the multimedia work from others, then you cannot put it into public domain unless, or until, you obtain permission from the owners of the content pieces.

DOCUMENTATION AND LICENSES

Question: I'm planning on giving credit to everyone from whom I borrow for my PowerPoint project. I believe that since I am citing the owners and showcasing their work, I will not need to purchase any licenses or obtain any permissions for using these works. Am I right?

Answer: No! You are wrong! By giving credit, you will not be committing plagiarism. However, you still could be in copyright violation. Copyright owners tend to see multimedia works as another area of sale. The same rules apply as for borrowing any copyrighted works (Brinson and Radcliffe, 1994).

Question: Can I, as a teacher, produce my own computer-based presentation for class instruction using a combination of student and commercial works?

Answer: Use the flow chart in Figure 11-3 to determine which materials you can use in your presentation.

Question: What is the first sale doctrine? How does it affect multimedia works?

Answer: The first sale doctrine gives the owner of a particular copy of a work the right to dispose of that copy as she or he sees fit (Duke Law and Technology Review, 2001). This means that someone who purchases a "lawfully made" computer-generated presentation has the right to display it, keep it, re-sell it, give it away, or toss it. However, the owner of the copy does not have the right to make copies

Figure 11–3
Using Student and Commercial Works in Computer-Based Presentations

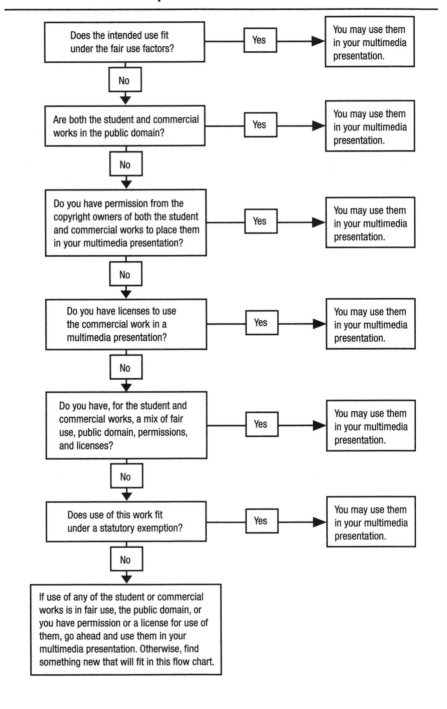

of his or her one copy, prepare derivative works, permit other borrowing of the work, or place the original in the public domain. Such rights are owned by the copyright holder of the original work.

Question: Imagine that you are an economics instructor for a class that is taught at two high schools, one site face-to-face and the other site via compressed video. You find a video in a vendor's catalog that fits the subject area of one of your class units. What really is appealing about this video is the catalog statement, which says that this video has copyright clearance to be used in both online and televised distance-education classes. You purchase the video and insert it into a multimedia project that you created for your class. Within a week, you have been contacted by the video's copyright owner. This person states that you have violated copyright law and must pay royalties to him for using his video for distance education. You point out the statement in the vendor's catalog, and the copyright owner tells you that it is a misprint. Have you really infringed on copyright law? Are you liable?

Answer: Yes, even though you used the work in good faith and according to the documentation that you found, you are in copyright violation. Cease using the video for distance education.[5]

PERMISSIONS

Question: Can an instructor show students' examples of multimedia projects to illustrate assessment concepts over a distance-education network?

Answer: Multimedia works can be used for face-to-face teaching, library reserve, and distance education (Warwick, 2001).[6] For distance-education courses, certain criteria must be met, as illustrated in Figure 11-4.

Question: How can I get permission to use an animation for a multimedia presentation when the animation is credited "from the Internet"?

Answer: You can't. Find another animation for which permission is available or the copyright owner identified, or both (and then ask for permission).

Question: If you write for permission to use a newspaper cartoon in a multimedia presentation and don't get a response, can you use the cartoon in your project if you cite the work?

Figure 11–4
Using Student Examples in Distance Education

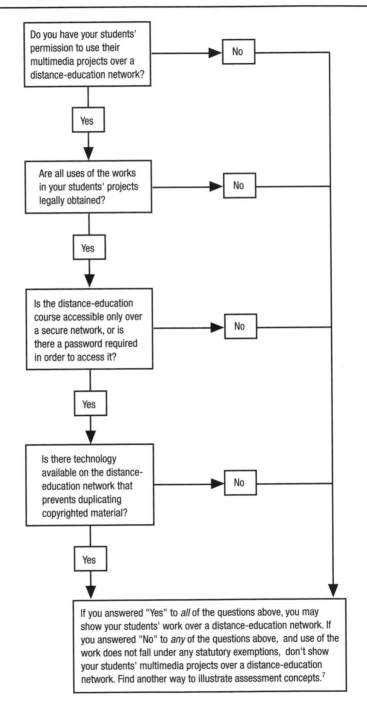

Do you have your students' permission to use their multimedia projects over a distance-education network? → No

Yes

Are all uses of the works in your students' projects legally obtained? → No

Yes

Is the distance-education course accessible only over a secure network, or is there a password required in order to access it? → No

Yes

Is there technology available on the distance-education network that prevents duplicating copyrighted material? → No

Yes

If you answered "Yes" to *all* of the questions above, you may show your students' work over a distance-education network. If you answered "No" to *any* of the questions above, and use of the work does not fall under any statutory exemptions, don't show your students' multimedia projects over a distance-education network. Find another way to illustrate assessment concepts.[7]

Answer: No, you cannot legally do so. By citing the work, you will not have plagiarized, however.

YOU CREATE IT, YOU OWN IT

Question: Somebody already copyrighted the name that I wanted to use for my multimedia project. Can I still use it?

Answer: Names cannot be copyrighted. Therefore, you can use a name, unless it is trademarked.[8]

Question: I created a very detailed multimedia project for a home economics class that I teach. I am now moving to a new district, and I want to take my project with me. My current school district says that I have to leave it with them. Who should get control of my multimedia project?

Answer: Use the flow chart in Figure 11-5 to determine if you own the project or if it is work for hire.

Question: I want to protect my ownership of a multimedia project that I created and presented over real-time television to a middle school class in another state. What do I need to do?

Answer: Register it with the U.S. Copyright Office. (See chapter 1.)

INFRINGEMENTS AND PENALTIES

Question: How do I know if I am allowed to use Internet clip art in my multimedia project?

Answer: Use the flow chart in Figure 11-6 to answer this question.

Question: I teach online. May I place an instructional video in my multimedia presentation for class?

Answer: Use the flow chart in Figure 11-7 to determine if you are allowed to use the video.

Question: Can I change a digitized image enough that it becomes my work, and I can place it in my multimedia production without worrying about copyright infringement?

Answer: No. A derivative work is a derivative work.

Question: Two of my seventh-grade students are Harry Potter fanatics. They have created a HyperStudio presentation about the

Figure 11–5
Who Owns Teacher-Created Multimedia?

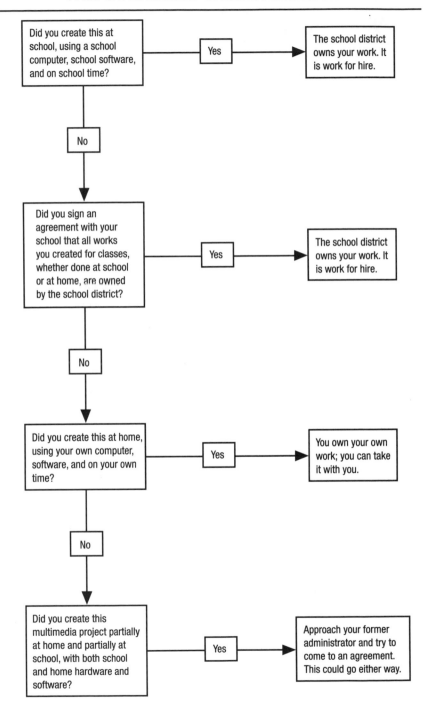

Figure 11–6
Using Clip Art in Multimedia Projects

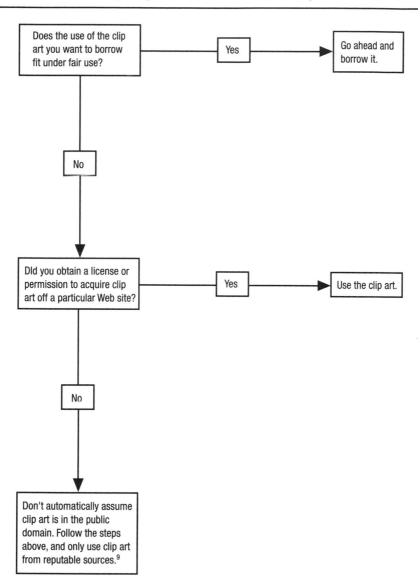

Figure 11–7
Using Videos in Multimedia Projects

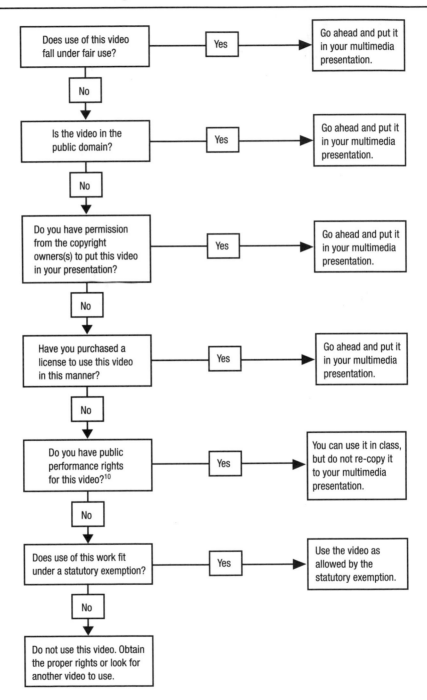

boy wizard, including a listing of links to a number of Web sites with Harry Potter–related domain names. I have heard that such Web sites violate copyright law, and I don't want them to get into any trouble. What's the deal here?

Answer: It is not a copyright violation if your students make their own list of Harry Potter *links* and put them in their HyperStudio presentation. However, Warner Bros. (WB) has legal ownership of Harry Potter–related domain names. Therefore, if your students wanted to create a new Harry Potter page, they would need to contact WB. It is possible to work out an agreement with WB so they either sponsor your site or allow you to run your own site (Healy, 2001; "Time Warner Gets 'Potter,'" 2000).

INTERNATIONAL COPYRIGHT LAW

Question: I am a history teacher. As part of a class multimedia presentation, I have created a list of links to historical sites worldwide. If I put the presentation on my Web page and make my links "live," will my students be copyright compliant if they use the links?

Answer: Yes. However, it would be good "netiquette" to ask for permission from those sites before you provide their links to your students.[11]

AVOIDING COPYRIGHT PROBLEMS

Question: One of my sixth graders wants to obtain copyright registration for the multimedia project he did in art class. Can he do so, since he is underage?

Answer: Sure he can. The U.S. Copyright Office "issues registrations to minors" as well as adults for copyright purposes (U.S. Copyright Office, 2003b, 1).

CONCLUSION

It is important to remember that the more you borrow without obtaining permission from the owner/creator of a work, the greater the likelihood that you might be in infringement of copyright law.[12] It does not matter what the work's format is. However, because a multimedia product may contain a number and variety of formats as part of its whole, obtaining the needed rights for use can be complicated and time consuming.

END NOTES

1. The copyright law is rather vague, as has been discussed in previous chapters, and is thus, open to interpretation. What this means is that, although the use described in this question constitutes a fair use, there is never an absolute guarantee.

2. Obtaining permission of the subjects of a photograph is a privacy issue, not a copyright one. However, it is a matter that should be addressed when using photographs for multimedia and other presentations, projects, and publications.

3. Reminder: Under Section 107 of the U.S. Copyright Law (1976), the four fair use factors are "(1) the purpose and character of the use, including whether such use is of a commercial nature or is for nonprofit educational purposes; (2) the nature of the copyrighted work; (3) the amount and substantiality of the portion used in relation to the copyrighted work as a whole; and (4) the effect of the use upon the potential market for or value of the copyrighted work." You can find the law in a number of places, including Copyright Office's Web site at <www.copyright.gov>.

4. In the preamble to the "Fair Use Guidelines for Educational Multimedia," the authors make the following observations, "While only the courts can authoritatively determine whether a particular use is fair use, these guidelines represent the participants' consensus of conditions under which fair use should generally apply and examples of when permission is required. Uses that exceed these guidelines neither may nor may not be fair use . . . the more one exceeds these guidelines, the greater the risk that fair use does not apply" (American Distance Education Consortium, 2003, preamble).

5. In such an instance, damages due to the copyright owner would probably be very minimal.

6. While all multimedia works can be used in these ways, they have the same limitations that are placed on uses of works in general. For example, does the use of the work fit under fair use, is the work in the public domain, does the borrower have permission or a license for such use, etc.

7. Please see discussion of the TEACH Act in chapter 13.

8. Trademarks distinguish "one product or service from another,

such as symbols, logos, sounds, designs . . ." (Hefter and Litowitz, n.d., 3).

9. In many instances Web pages provide clip art to users. While currently clip art is most often in the form of images, animations and sound can also be clip art. The problem is that sometimes those creating or owning the Web page could borrow copyrighted images, etc., from other sites, place these on their site, and then inform users that the site is in the public domain. Unless you know more about a piece of clip art, you might not know whether it is really in the public domain or not. Therefore, when using clip art that has been identified as public-domain material, it is best to obtain it from a site that you consider reputable, such as a prominent computer software site.

10. Purchasing public performance rights can be considered purchasing a license to use the work publicly.

11. It may not always be practical, on the other hand, to ask for permission to link to others' Internet sites. You will need to use your own judgment on this issue.

12. Sometimes all that the owner/creator wants is recognition for his or her work. Therefore, on all your educational multimedia creations (and other creations as well) remember to include a reference section at the beginning, end, or in the body of your work, where you cite those from whom you have obtained material.

REFERENCES

American Distance Education Consortium. 2003. "Fair Use Guidelines for Educational Multimedia." Lincoln, NE. (June). Available: www.adec.edu/admin/papers/fair10-17.html (accessed June 7, 2004).

Brinson, J. Dianne, and Mark F. Radcliffe. 1994. "Intellectual Property Law Primer for Multimedia Developers." Oakland: Timestream. Available: www.timestream.com/stuff/neatstuff/mmlaw.html (accessed June 7, 2004).

Congressional Management Foundation. (2004) "Congressional Online Project. Glossary." (March). Available: www.congressonlineproject.org/glossary.html (accessed June 7, 2004).

Davis, Melissa. "Copywrite Free Music." Splendora, TX: Splendora Middle School. (23 February 1998) LM_NET Archives.

Duke Law and Technology Review. 2001. "The First Sale Doctrine and Digital Phonorecords." Raleigh, NC. (May). Available: www.law.duke.edu/journals/dltr/articles/2001dltr0018.html (accessed June 7, 2004).

Healy, Christopher. 2001. "Potter's Posse: Web Site Wizards Fight Off Corporate Muggles." *Teen People* (November): 143.

Hefter, Laurence, and Robert D. Litowitz. n.d. "What Is Intellectual Property?" Washington, DC: Finnegan, Henderson, Farabow, Garrett & Dunner. Available: http://usinfo.state.gov/products/pubs/intelprp/ (accessed June 7, 2004).

Hoffman, Ivan. 2000. "The Use of Protected Materials in Multimedia Corporate Training and Distance Education Projects." Available: www.ivanhoffman.com/protected2.html (accessed June 7, 2004).

Russell, Carrie. 2003. "Sound Advice: Can Students Edit Pop CDs as Part of a Multimedia Class?" *School Library Journal* 49, no. 11 (November): 3.

Talab, Rosemary S. 1997. "Copyright and You: An Educational Use Checklist for Copyright and Multimedia." *TechTrends* 42, no. 1 (January/February): 9–11.

"Time Warner Gets 'Potter.'" 2000. *Chicago Tribune*. (December 29), sec. 5, 8.

U.S. Code. 2001. Section 107. "Limitations on Exclusive Rights: Fair Use." Washington, DC: U.S. Copyright Office.

U.S. Copyright Office. 2003a. "FAQ: Assignment/Transfer of Copyright Ownership." (April). Available: www.copyright.gov/help/faq/faq-assignment.html (accessed June 7, 2004).

———. 2003b. "FAQ: Who Can Register?" (April). Available: www.copyright.gov/help/faq/faq-who.html (accessed June 7, 2004).

Warwick, Shelly. 2001. "Copyright Issues in Presentations and Other Multimedia Works." *TechTrends* 45, no. 5 (September/October): 3–6.

Chapter Twelve

Print Works and Copyright Law: Is It OK to Copy Print Works for Class at the Last Minute?

INTRODUCTION

Print, as a medium, covers a very large area: books, newspapers, magazines, poetry, play scripts, cartoons, recipes, and so on. When copying or borrowing from print sources, it is important to be aware not only of the fair use factors, but also of the brevity, spontaneity, and cumulative effect test.[1] These three "tests" are guidelines, endorsed by the United States Congress, for purposes of educational and classroom copying (print), and are interpreted from the 1976 Copyright Act. Basically, what they do is help interpret application of the fair use factors. "Brevity" means the least amount possible is to be copied. This amounts to a whole poem if the poem is less than 250 words or an excerpt from a poem of no more than 250 words; 2,500 words or less for an essay or article, or no more than 10% or 1,000 words for an excerpt; or one illustration per book or periodical. "Spontaneity" means that the copying is a "last-minute" request for class, instigated by an individual instructor. "Cumulative effect" means the amount of work that is copied over a class term. For print material that is as follows. (1) "The copying of the material is for only one course in the school in which the copies are made." (2) "Not more than one short poem, article, story, essay or two excerpts may be copied from the same author, nor more than three from the same collective work or periodical volume during one class term." (3) "There shall not be more than nine instances of such multiple copying for one course during one class term," and "The limitations stated in (2) and (3) above shall not apply to current news periodicals and newspapers and current news sections of other periodicals" (Association of American Publishers, n.d.).[2]

Below are questions that cover print, educators, and copyright. Questions with more than one answer are presented in flow chart form. Remember, when you use the flow charts in this chapter, you are trying to find any criterion under which you may borrow a work. Therefore, you need only follow each flow chart until you come to that point where you satisfy one of the criteria. Once you reach that point, there is no need to go any further. For more information on each area discussed, please refer to the chapter (in part I) in which that particular subject is covered.

FAIR USE

Question: I teach biology. I have a textbook that I would like my students to read. However, it is very expensive, and the school has decided that they will not purchase it for my class. Can I photocopy parts of the book for each member of class?

Answer: Use the flow chart in Figure 12-1 to determine if you are allowed to make these copies.

Question: One of my students has visual problems and can only read large print. Can I copy the social studies textbook for my student using the enlarging feature on the copy machine?

Answer: If the book is not available in large print (or in some other way that makes it usable by the visually impaired student, such as a book-on-tape), then copying it for your student comes under fair use. However, there are a number of companies that make large print copies of textbooks. There are also machines, such as the closed-circuit television (CCTV) and small hand-held magnifiers, that enlarge print. Pursue these options before enlarging a textbook for your student. Also, if you have purchased a large print textbook and it is not yet available, some companies will let you make an enlarged copy to use until the commercial one arrives (Brisco, 2003).[3]

Question: Does copying one illustration from a picture book fall under fair use?

Answer: Because it is a picture book, that is, there are many illustrations in the book, one copy of one illustration would fall under

Figure 12–1
Photocopying Parts of a Book

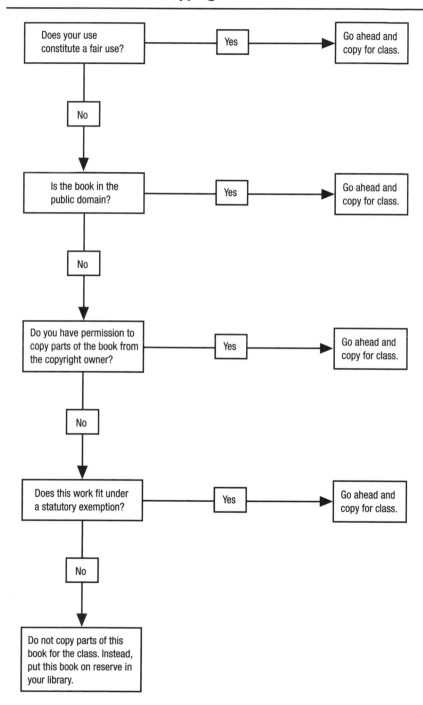

Figure 12–2
Copying Textbooks for Visually Impaired Students

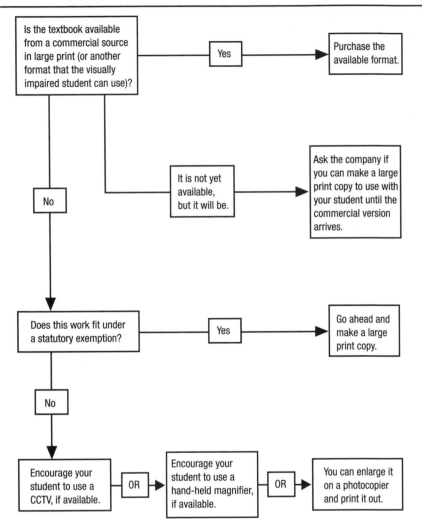

the fair use factors *unless* each illustration is registered for copyright separately. Of course, be sure to check if any of the statutory exemptions for classrooms, libraries, or archives apply. In that case, copying one illustration from a picture book could be an infringement. Check on the verso (back) of the page. Information on the illustrations' copyright should be there.[4]

PUBLIC DOMAIN

Question: There is a chapter in a book that I would really like to use in my class. I have tried contacting the publisher, but the company doesn't seem to exist anymore. Does that mean that this book is now in the public domain?

Answer: Use the flow chart in Figure 12-3 to determine if the book is in the public domain.

Question: If a magazine is out-of-print, is it now in the public domain and thus, is it legal for me to make copies of one of the articles for my class?

Answer: It is important to recognize here, that as a rule, each *article* is independently protected by its own copyright registration. Thus, you must check copyright registration for the article you wish. (See also the flow chart in Figure 12-4.)

DOCUMENTATION AND LICENSES

Question: As the school librarian, do I need public performance rights to read a storybook to an elementary class? I know that librarians do this all the time. Are we all copyright infringers?

Answer: Well, the book is being used in a public performance, in a school setting. Assuming that the school is nonprofit, that the performance is occurring in the library or another place dedicated to instruction, and that the storybook was legally obtained, then, yes, you can read the book and not be infringing on someone's copyright (U.S. Copyright Law, 1976). It is also possible that such a reading fits under the four fair use factors. Furthermore, ". . . there are general practices that we have come to accept as OK. These practices have become so normalized that they actually affect the development and interpretation of the copyright law" (Russell, 2003a). Therefore, yes, you can read a storybook to a class without public performance rights.

Question: We do not have enough scripts for our senior class play. Is there any problem with copying a couple more for the student directors?

Answer: Yes, there is a problem! The theater teacher or whoever produces the play usually signs a contract with a licensing agency

Figure 12–3
Books in the Public Domain

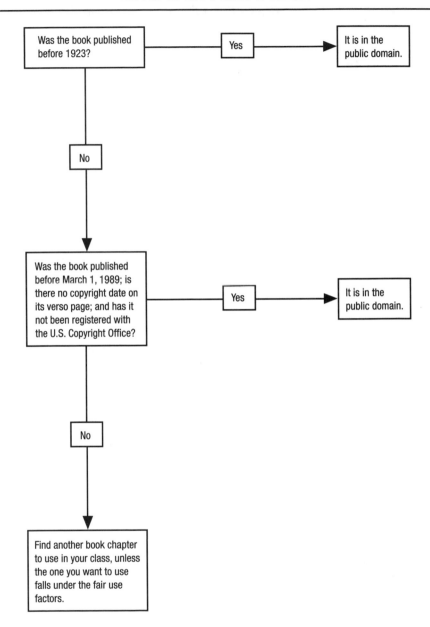

Figure 12–4
Magazine Articles in the Public Domain

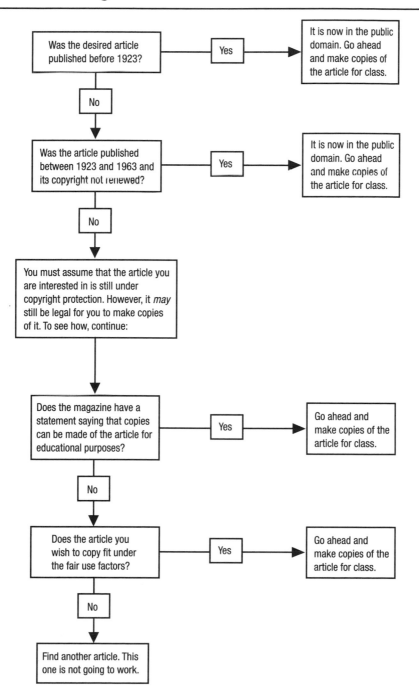

as to which rights have been purchased and which have not. The school then pays royalties to the agency for those rights purchased. Purchased rights can include the number of times the play may be put on in public, the dates between which the play may be put on, the amount and type of advertising that may be done, whether you can make changes to the script or not (most licenses exclude the making of script changes), or even the copying of scripts. First check the terms of the license you have signed. Your question on copying the script a couple more times may be answered there. If it is not, it is best to ask the licensing agency for permission to copy the scripts, if more are needed (Scott, 2000).

Question: We are in the process of putting on a play. How many times can we give public performances of it? We are charging admission.

Answer: The contract the school signs with the licensing agency will determine how many times the play may be performed in public.

Question: I want to copy a magazine article 30 times for a class reading assignment. Can I do this under copyright law?

Answer: Use the flow chart in Figure 12-5 to determine if the copyright law allows copying this article.

Question: I found a clip-art workbook with free copyright designs in it. I may use this any way I want, right?

Answer: You may use the clip art in any way that the workbook says you can. For instance, the statement on the back side of the front cover of *Ready-to-Use Old-Fashioned Illustrations of Books, Reading & Writing*, states that the purchaser of the workbook may use the "designs and illustrations for graphics and crafts applications, free and without special permission, provided that you include no more than ten in the same publication or project" (Grafton, 1992, i). In addition, it gives an address to contact for permission for more use as well as the following: ". . . republication or reproduction of any illustration by any other graphic service whether it be in a book or in any other design resource is strictly prohibited" (Grafton, 1992, i). So, read the documentation on your resource, no matter if it says "free" or not.

Figure 12–5
Making Multiple Copies of Articles

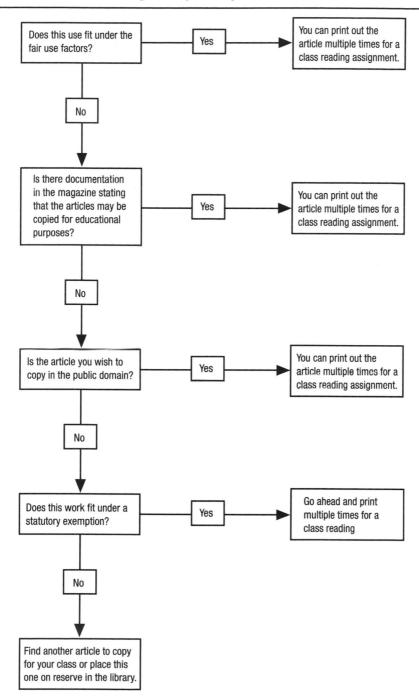

PERMISSIONS

Question: The principal just brought a new student to my class. I don't have another workbook for him to use. Am I allowed to copy workbook pages off another student's for my new student to use?

Answer: Use the flow chart in Figure 12-6 to determine if you are allowed to copy the workbook.

Question: I'd like to start my class computer-based presentation by digitizing a current political cartoon from the local newspaper and inserting it onto the first slide. Is doing this OK?[5]

Answer: The flow chart in Figure 12-7 will help you decide if you are allowed to use the cartoon this way.

YOU CREATE IT, YOU OWN IT

Question: Our parent–teacher organization (PTO) wants to do a cookbook as a fund-raiser. Students, faculty, and parents will bring in their favorite recipes, and these will be compiled into a school cookbook. Are recipes copyrighted?

Answer: According to the U.S. Copyright Office, "listings of ingredients as in recipes . . . are not subject to copyright protection. However, where a recipe . . . is accompanied by substantial literary expression in the form of an explanation or directions, or when there is a combination of recipes, as in a cookbook, there may be a basis for copyright protection" (U.S. Copyright Office, 1999).[6] What this means for the school PTO is that recipes out of other cookbooks should not be used. Therefore, the recipes for the school cookbook either need to be original to the students, faculty, and parents donating them or they need to be generic; i.e., lists of ingredients and basic steps to putting them together—without any additional creativity or originality (U.S. Copyright Office, 2003). Moreover, the PTO can officially register the cookbook with the U.S. Copyright Office. (Remember, under U.S. copyright law, that the cookbook is copyrighted even if it is not registered with the U.S. Copyright Office.)

Question: The eighth-grade science teachers want to put together their own curriculum. Can they use flow charts and simple Venn diagrams obtained from a commercial science manual?

Figure 12–6
Copying Workbook Pages

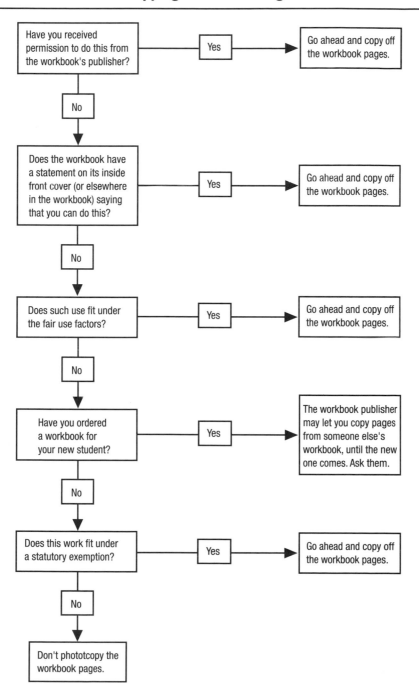

Figure 12–7
Digitizing Newspaper Cartoons

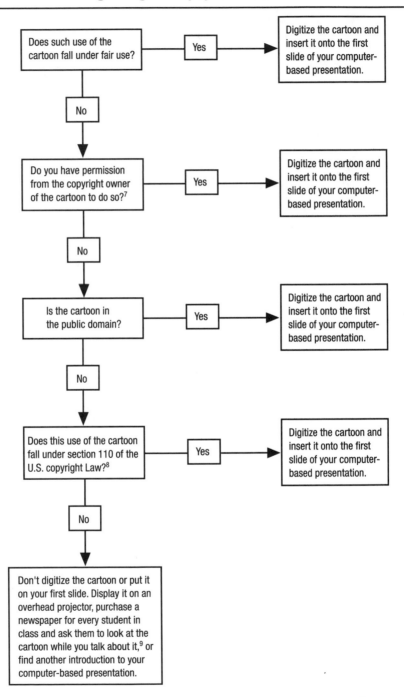

Answer: Like recipes, flow charts and diagrams can only be protected by copyright law when they have a considerable amount of originality to them. Basically, the form—unless unusual enough to be considered a work of art—cannot be protected. In addition, the content must convey original information in order for it to be copyrighted. Flow charts and Venn diagrams that basically illustrate procedures or processes cannot be copyrighted (personal communication from Copyright Office, 2003; Quinn, 2003). Since it is highly likely that the flow charts and diagrams in the science manual are simple procedural works, they can be used by the science teachers. However, the bottom line is that the science teachers, themselves, will have to study the flow charts and Venn diagrams and make their own interpretations. If they determine that the flow charts and Venn diagrams are original enough to be copyrighted, then they need to contact the copyright owners of the commercial science manual and ask for permission to use their works.

Question: I am the middle school art teacher. One of my students is amazingly talented. She won a state award for one of her paintings, which she then sold to a local business. The local business has created postcards of her painting, which they plan to sell. The business says that since they bought her painting, they own the copyright to it. I say that the student owns the copyright, and that the business must pay royalties if they print up postcards of that painting. Who is right?

Answer: You are. Unless the student consciously transferred the copyright to the painting to the local business, she still owns said copyright. (Remember, transfer of the copyright requires a written document/contract.) Thus, the local business owns the specific painting; it does not own the rights to make derivatives of it or to make copies of it. And, in all likelihood, they have already infringed on her exclusive rights (copyright) by creating the postcards.

INFRINGEMENTS AND PENALTIES

Question: Is it a copyright infringement if my class uses clip art off the Internet to design book covers for a class unit?

Answer: In order to protect your class from copyright infringement, direct them to use clip art only from reputable Internet sites, such as sites for which the school has purchased a license to use. Also instruct them to follow the documentation on those sites.

Question: Help! Class starts in 10 minutes, and I need a poem! There is a poem that will work in one of my teacher's manuals. Can I copy it for all members of my class? After all, it is a last minute thing.

Answer: The flow chart in Figure 12-8 will help you determine if you can make the copies.

INTERNATIONAL COPYRIGHT LAW

Question: One of the high school English classes is studying *Beowolf.* Mr. Smith, the English teacher, has found an excellent article on this subject, published in a British journal, that he would like to share with his fellow English teachers, districtwide. How can he easily—and legally—provide his colleagues with a copy?

Answer: This answer can get complicated. (1) If use of the article falls under fair use, the article is in the public domain, Mr. Smith has permission or a license from the copyright owner to copy the article, or there is a disclaimer in the magazine saying (something to the effect) that the articles in it can be copied "for educational purposes," (and his use fits the disclaimer), it will be easy for him to share the *Beowolf* article districtwide. (Remember, since the U.S. belongs to several copyright treaty organizations, it is simplest to treat the work as you would under U.S. law.) (2) If none of the above is the case, he could ask one of the school libraries to put *his* copy of the article on reserve, for other teachers to use. (3) In addition, the "Guidelines Conforming to Fair Use for Educational Purposes Agreement on Guidelines for Classroom Copying"[10] say that a teacher may make or have made a *single* copy of an article, chapter, short story, poem, essay (or a diagram or picture in any of the above works) (Torrans, 2003). Thus, if following these guidelines, Mr. Smith could make one copy of the article for his use (or request that one copy of the article be made for him). (4) Moreover, under section 108(a) of the 1976 Copyright Act, a library may make one copy of a work if (a) there is no commercial advantage (direct or indirect) to making another copy; (b) the library collection is open to the public, especially researchers; and (c) the copy of the original work includes on it either a copyright notice or a statement saying the work may be under copyright protection. So, each of the English teachers could ask the library to make a copy for him or her. Are you getting confused yet? Well, all of the above

Figure 12–8
Last-Minute Copying

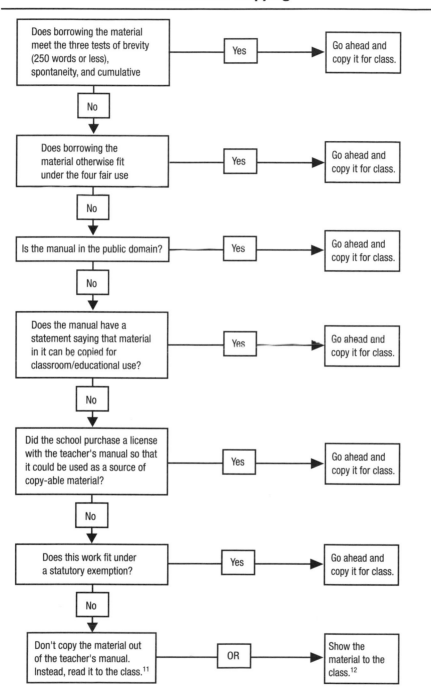

may apply, depending on your situation. (5) The easiest way for Mr. Smith to get this information to his fellow English teachers districtwide is to route it (send it from teacher to teacher through the interdistrict mail)![13]

AVOIDING COPYRIGHT PROBLEMS

Answer: Can school media specialists use copied or scanned images of book covers on bulletin boards and in displays? After all, by doing so we're providing free advertising for the books.

Answer: This question has both a conservative and a liberal answer.

Conservative: According to the basic interpretation of copyright law, this is an infringement. Why? Because it means that you are copying works in an unauthorized manner. In other words, you need to obtain the proper permissions. Or, you can put the *actual* book covers on your bulletin boards and in your displays.

Liberal: The copying or scanning of book covers fits under the fair use factors. You may copy or scan them for use on bulletin boards and in displays.[14]

CONCLUSION

While print has been around longer than many other formats, such as computer software and digital recordings, the same sorts of copyright questions keep popping up. How much is too much? What is legal and what isn't? How can we copy and not be liable? Confusing? You bet! This chapter tries very hard to give you a definitive answer. However, in some cases, such an answer simply does not exist. Indeed, I hope that this chapter provides you with usable answers to some of your copyright questions.

END NOTES

1. The "brevity, spontaneity, and cumulative effect test" is sometimes called the "three print tests" in schools.
2. It is possible for print copying to fall under the fair use factors but not under the brevity, spontaneity, and cumulative effect tests' rule (National Association of College Stores [NACS], 2004). Therefore, while both are addressed in this chapter, be aware that if your use of a work falls under fair use, you don't need to worry about the "brevity, spontaneity, and cumulative effect test."

3. Although it does not apply to the specific situation in Figure 12-2, section 121 of the U.S. Copyright Law is important to educators when working with blind and other students with disabilities. This section sets forth limits on the exclusive rights of copyright holders when reproducing works for people who are visually impaired and people with other disabilities. (See Appendices III–V.)

4. If the information you are looking for is not on the verso, or elsewhere in the book, you need to go through the basic steps we discuss in this book, including checking to see if the item is in the public domain, and if not, searching for permission to use it. In such a case, a clearinghouse for print materials (see chapter 4) would come in handy.

5. In addition to following the flow chart in Figure 12-7, you may want to consider the first sale doctrine. This doctrine, rooted in contract law (Torrans, 2003), basically states that the owner of a particular copy of a work has the right to dispose of that copy as she or he sees fit (Duke Law and Technology Review, 2001). This means that if you purchased the political cartoon legally, then you have the right to display it, keep it, re-sell it, give it away, or toss it. *However*, you do not have the right to make copies of your one copy, prepare derivative works, permit other borrowing of the work, or place the original in the public domain. Because in this instance, you wished to make a digital *copy* of the cartoon, the first sale doctrine, here, is "iffy" at best.

6. A *compilation* of recipes, generic enough individually to be nonprotected under copyright law, can be copyrighted. It is similar to the discussion in chapter 6 in which there is a discussion of how links can be in the public domain, but *lists* of links can be protected under copyright law.

7. The copyright owner of a newspaper cartoon is usually a syndicate, such as United Media, which acts as a vendor for the cartoonist, contacting newspapers, handling royalties, and working with contracts and licenses. A few cartoonists own their own cartoons (Besenjak, 1997).

8. Section 110(1) of the Copyright Law says that it is not an infringement for a teacher to display a work in a nonprofit education setting (classroom) if the copy was lawfully made. Section 110(2) adds the following, which may affect the display if you are transmitting it: if the display is a regular part of the instructional activities; if the display is directly related/or material is of assistance to the teaching content of the transmission; and if the transmission of the

work is made for classroom reception or for people with disabilities or other circumstances that prevent their attendance in the classroom; then—it is not an infringement to use it (U.S. Copyright Law, 1976).

9. As a former K-12 teacher, I do understand the impracticality of purchasing a newspaper for every student in class. However, it is an option in this case.

10. These guidelines were made part of the *Congressional Record* in 1976. "Following these guidelines generally demonstrates that a good faith effort has been made to comply with the copyright law" (Torrans, 2003, 75). However, bottom line, these are *not* law; they are guidelines only and should be treated as such.

11. Reading the poem to the class is allowable under section 110 of the U.S. Copyright Law.

12. For example, the teacher's manual copy of the poem could be passed around to all class members or displayed in the room for easy access by the students.

13. The Guidelines for Classroom Copying in Not-For-Profit Educational Institutions with Respect to Books and Periodicals maintain that teachers may retain articles in their files for research, teaching, or personal purposes (NACS, 204). This is true in many cases; however, be aware that all lawmakers are not in agreement with such a stance.

14. According to Carrie Russell (2002), the American Library Association's copyright specialist, this is another case in which, because the action is so commonplace, it changes how copyright law is understood. As long as the library media specialists are not charging entrance to the media center or in some other way obtaining proceeds from the copied book cover displays, such displays become exceptions to the law; i.e., they promote reading and have only a positive influence on the marketplace. Thus, such displays fit under the four fair use factors.

REFERENCES

Association of American Publishers. n.d. "Conferences & Publications: Publications—Guidelines for Classroom Copying: Agreement on Guidelines for Classroom Copying in Not-For-Profit Educational Institutions with Respect to Books and Periodicals." Washington, DC. Association of American Publishers. Available: www.publishers.org/conference/pubinfo.cfm?PublicationID=3.

Besenjak, Cheryl. 1997. *Copyright Plain & Simple.* Franklin Lakes, NJ: Career.

Duke Law and Technology Review. 2001. "The First Sale Doctrine and Digital Phonorecords." (0018, May 31). Available: www.law.duke.edu/journals/dltr/articles/2001dltr0018.html (accessed June 7, 2004).

Grafton, Carol Belanger. 1992. *Ready-to-Use: Old-Fashioned Illustrations of Books, Reading & Writing.* New York: Dover.

IPWatchdog.com. 2003. "The Law of Recipes." Nashua. Available: www.ipwatchdog.com/recipes.html (accessed June 7, 2004).

National Association of College Stores (NACS). 2004. "Industry Information: Questions and Answers for the Campus Community." Oberlin, OH: NACS. Available: www.nacs.org/public/copyright/appendix/asp (accessed June 10, 2004).

Russell, Carrie. 2002. "Is It a Crime to Copy?" *School Library Journal* 48, no. 1 (January): 41.

———. 2003a. "A Get-Rich-Quick Scheme? Your School's Fund-Raiser May Not Qualify for a Copyright Exemption." *School Library Journal* 49, no. 2 (February): 43.

———. 2003b. "A More Manageable Harry: Is It Legal to Circulate Small Sections of the Latest 'Harry Potter'?" *School Library Journal* 49, no. 9 (September): 43.

———. 2003c. "A Tale of Two Formats: Is It Legal to Make DVD Copies of Instructional Videos?" *School Library Journal* 49, no. 4 (April): 45.

Scott, Kevin N. 2000. "Who Owns the Rights? Copyright, the Law and Licensing the Show." Cincinnati: Educational Theatre Association. (February). Available: www.angelfire.com/or/Copyright4Producers/intro.html (accessed June 7, 2004).

Simpson, Carol. 2001. *Copyright for Schools: A Practical Guide*, 3rd ed. Worthington: Linworth.

Torrans, Lee Ann. 2003. *Law for K-12 Libraries and Librarians.* Westport, OH: Libraries Unlimited.

U.S. Copyright Law. 1976. Washington, DC. Public Law 94-553, sec. 110.

U.S. Copyright Office. 1999. "Recipes." (June). Available: www.copyright.gov/fls/fl122.html (accessed June 11, 2004).

Chapter Thirteen

Distance Learning and Copyright Law: Is This Different From Applying Copyright Law in a Face-to-Face Classroom?

INTRODUCTION

Distance education in K-12 schools is not as common as it is in institutions of higher learning, and in many elementary and secondary schools it is being used in a simpler manner (MacDonald, 1997) than that exhibited in academia. However for both groups, when it comes to copyright law and learning in a non-face-to-face environment, there is confusion and dissension. Today, distance education comprises Web-based delivery, asynchronous communications, and television transmissions, and others forms of delivery. Distance education must either abide by the Technology, Education and Copyright Harmonization Act (TEACH Act)[1] or rely on the fair use factors (discussed in chapter 2). Unhappily for us as users, federal legislation is often confusing. Therefore, the TEACH Act is briefly summarized below, with focus on the K-12 environment.

TECHNOLOGY, EDUCATION, AND COPYRIGHT HARMONIZATION ACT (TEACH ACT)

Educators who apply the TEACH Act, support a much more liberal interpretation of copyright use and access of materials than old section 110(2) of the Copyright Act.[2] The TEACH Act was written to update "the existing distance learning exception to the Copyright Act to accommodate the growth of *digital age* distance learning" (American Association of Community Colleges, 2002).[3] This act

> expands existing "face-to-face" teaching exemptions in the copyright law to allow teachers at accredited, nonprofit educational institutions throughout the U.S. to use copyright-protected materials in distance education—including on Web sites and by other digital means—without prior permission from the copyright owner and without payment of royalties (American Libraries Online, 2002, 1).

In order to use the TEACH Act, your educational organization needs to follow a long list of requirements. All of these criteria must be met.

Requirements of the TEACH Act to Be Met by All Institutions Using It

INSTITUTIONAL RESPONSIBILITIES

The institution must:

- be an accredited nonprofit institution,
- have a copyright policy,
- provide copyright information to its faculty, students, and staff,
- provide notice to students that all distance education materials may be copyright protected, and
- limit class access to students enrolled in it.

INFORMATION TECHNOLOGY RESPONSIBILITIES

Those who work with the information technologies that support distance education in your organization must:

- limit access to students enrolled in a specific class,
- apply technological controls on storage and dissemination to prevent course students from retaining the material for longer than a class session,
- assure that the distance education delivery systems used don't defeat technological measures used by copyright owners to keep their works under control,
- limit short-term retention of copies, and
- limit long-term copies' preservation.

INSTRUCTOR RESPONSIBILITIES

The distance education course instructors must:

- use only works exclusively permitted,

- not use works clearly disqualified,
- supervise all course materials' access,
- mediate all instructional activities,
- ensure that no digital versions of a work are available,[4]
- corroborate the specific material and amount of said material to be digitized,[5] and
- evaluate access control implications.[6] (American Library Association [ALA], 2002)[7]

Many educational organizations have adopted guidelines for their distance education programs that are similar to some of the TEACH Act requirements (Harper, 2001; Gilbert, 1999).

Abiding by the numerous terms of the TEACH Act can be difficult. Because of this, many institutions elect to follow the fair use factors instead. Either set of rules can be followed, just not both.

Working with distance-education copyright issues is extremely complicated and beyond the scope of this book. In fact, it could be a whole book in its own right. However, the flow chart in Figure 13-1 will give distance educators an idea of which set of rules they should abide by: the TEACH Act or the fair use factors.

CONCLUSION

As more and more elementary and secondary schools use distance-delivery systems to support curriculum and student needs, copyright rules will be challenged and new limits set. At present, copyright law's intersection with distance education is very complex.

END NOTES

1. There is another act, the Digital Millennium Copyright Act (DMCA), that also affects distance education. Specifically, its charge was to submit to Congress recommendations on promoting digital technologies in distance education. The DMCA-collected recommendations were submitted to Congress in 1999 (U.S. Copyright Office, 1999; Crews, 2000).

2. Section 110(2) of the Copyright Act: Instructional Broadcasting explains copyright coverage under the 1976 law. Covering classroom exemptions in light of face-to-face teaching, it was replaced by the TEACH Act. Section 110(2) is much more conservative than the TEACH Act, and much of it means little in light of digital trans-

Figure 13–1
Distance Educator's Flow Chart

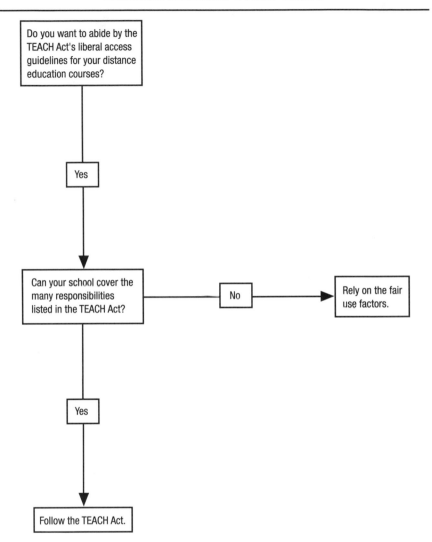

missions (Gasaway, 2002), which were not a consideration when this part of the Copyright Law was written.

3. The TEACH Act is actually a "new" (as of November 2002) Section 110(2).

4. Some copyright owners have been concerned with the idea that their analog materials could be converted to a digital format, thus making downloading and dissemination of their materials much easier. The concern is that owners' control over their materials

would become much more difficult. Therefore, the TEACH Act includes a statement that prohibits digital conversion of analog materials, *with some exceptions* (see end notes 5 and 6).

5. The first exception is that "the amount that may be converted is limited to the amount of appropriate works that may be performed or displayed, pursuant to the revised section 110(2)" (ALA, 2002, 7). What this means is that the distance education instructor needs to make sure that the material converted to digital format falls within the materials' scope and portion margins allowable under the TEACH Act (ALA, 2002).

6. The second exception is that teachers and other distance educators should check to make sure that there is not already a copy of the work they want to utilize in a digitized format, and if there is a digitized version, that it is available for use (ALA, 2002).

7. In addition to the responsibilities of the administration, technology coordinators and support people, and the class instructors, school library media specialists also find that they need to meet the TEACH Act requirements. The school library media specialists are poised, because of their training, to develop and interpret copyright and other access policies; store distance-education course transmissions; find other sources of materials for non-face-to-face class use; and so on. However, school library media specialists are not specifically listed in the TEACH Act (ALA, 2002).

REFERENCES

American Association of Community Colleges, et al. 2002. Letter to the Honorable Dennis J. Hastert, Speaker of the U.S. House of Representatives and the Honorable Richard A. Gephardt, Minority Leader, U.S. House of Representatives. (5 August) [signed by 38 groups and 4 individuals]. Available: www.educause.edu/ir/library/pdf/NET0319.pdf (accessed June 11, 2004).

American Libraries Online. 2002. "President Bush Signs Distance-Ed Copyright Bill" [News Archive]. (November 11). Available: www.ala.org/alaonline/currentnews/newsarchive/2002/november2002/presidentbush.htm (accessed June 11, 2004).

American Library Association (ALA) Washington Office. 2002. "The Technology, Education and Copyright Harmonization (TEACH) Act." (October). Available: www.ala.org/washoff/teach.html (accessed June 7, 2004).

Crews, Kenneth D. 2000. *Copyright Essentials for Librarians and Educators.* Chicago: American Library Association.

Gasaway, Laura N. 2002. "TEACH Act—Amended Section 110(2)." Chapel Hill: University of North Carolina. (November). Available: www.unc.edu/~unclng/TEACH.htm (accessed June 7, 2004).

Gilbert, Norden S. 1999. "Guidelines on Fair Use in Distance (On-line) Instruction" [Unpublished]. DeKalb: Northern Illinois University.

Harper, Georgia. 2001. "Copyright Law for Distance Ed." Presented at Northern Illinois University, Conference on Copyright and Intellectual Property Issues for Online Instruction, 28 September, DeKalb, IL.

MacDonald, Randall M. 1997. *The Internet and the School Library Media Specialist: Transforming Traditional Services*. Westport, CT: Greenwood.

U.S. Copyright Office. 2004. "Copyright Office Study on Distance Education." Available: www.copyright.gov/disted/ (accessed June 7, 2004).

Chapter Fourteen

Conclusion: What Does All This Mean for K-12 Teachers and Librarians?

INTRODUCTION

The first five chapters of this book focus on defining the most important issues within copyright for the K-12 teacher or librarian. Chapters 6 through 13 reflect on how teachers, school library media specialists, technology specialists, administrators, and others in the schools can best use copyright law in elementary, middle, and secondary school environments. This, the final chapter, covers options for avoiding copyright problems as well as how we can best work with those who would have us violate copyright law.

I'LL NEVER GET CAUGHT

Should you infringe on copyright law, it is possible that you will not be discovered. It is also possible that a software company, video company, or an organization representing whatever work you are copying will recognize that you are using their work illegally, and decide that it is not worth the time or money to prosecute. However, please be aware that, "…in some cases, software producers and distributors, as well as the organizations to which they belong, provide ways for consumers and concerned citizens to report cases of software piracy. Usually this can be done through the Internet or by phone, with the information kept confidential. In some cases, finders' fees may be available" (Butler, 2002, 42). The same holds true for video piracy and, depending on the organization, may also be applicable for other types of media. So, while you might not get caught, then again, you also might. Copyright infringement can be a felony. However, whether the infringement is judged to be criminal or civil, it is punishable by law. Penalties can include sizeable fines, payment of attorneys' fees, and even prison (It's Illegal to Violate Copyright Law, 1991). You must decide for yourself—is it worth the risk?

WAYS TO AVOID COPYRIGHT PROBLEMS

How can we avoid copyright problems? The best ways are to (1) understand copyright law, (2) stay current with its changes, and (3) follow the law's every nuance. However, in real life, copyright is just one small part of our teaching responsibilities. Therefore, practicing these three guidelines can be very hard to do. However, here are a few pointers to help you on your way to copyright compliance.

- Follow the fair use guidelines.
- Obtain permissions, licenses, and so on, when necessary.
- Always read documentation and other copyright information for each work you use or from which you borrow, and encourage others to do the same. This way you and other users will know what rights for a work are available under its license.
- Pay royalties as required.
- Consult your school district copyright policy or ethics code.[1] If your district does not have one, encourage your administration to develop one and follow its policies and procedures.
- Consult your school district attorney when questions and problems occur.
- Put the purpose and intended use on all purchase orders. This way, the publisher/vendor will know what you want the material for and can make sure that you obtain the licenses you need.
- Follow books, such as this one, that can help you answer copyright questions.
- Consult copyright articles in print journals and on the Web to be as up-to-date as you possibly can.
- Do not attempt to profit from your copying.
- Always cite what you quote. (Remember, citing is no substitute for permissions, licenses, etc. However, often copyright owners want credit for their works, and some—believe it or not—do not care as much about the monetary rewards. Thus, you can at least be careful not to plagiarize.)

- Participate in workshops and in-services that inform you about copyright law.
- Use material that you have created yourself.
- Observe and model responsible copyright practices.
- When in doubt, *don't copy!*

HOW TO DEAL WITH THOSE WHO WOULD HAVE YOU BREAK THE LAW

Unfortunately, there will always be some who believe that they are above the law. They may be your administrators, fellow teachers, students, and parents, almost anyone. How do you deal with someone—especially a person who is technically your supervisor—who asks you to infringe on another individual's or group's copyrights?

How to Deal with a Supervisor Who Wants You to Copy Illegally

Question: Pretend that you are the special education teacher. You have just found an excellent article on teaching devices for deaf students, which you point out to your principal. The principal tells you to photocopy this article 25 times, for all the teachers in the school, and then put it in their mailboxes. This way, everyone can obtain this information. You notice on the inside front cover of the periodical from which the article came a statement saying that no copying of material from the periodical is to occur without permission of the publishers. You point this out to the principal, who informs you to do what you were told anyway. What do you do?

Answer: Well, especially if you are new and untenured, you might just (1) copy the article 25 times and put it in all the teachers' mailboxes. Chances are that no one will be the wiser. You could also (2) choose to confront the administrator on this issue and say "no," although this option might jeopardize your relationship with him or her. A better idea would be (3) to give the principal a brief rundown on copyright law and why it is important to not be in violation. You might also be able (4) to persuade the principal that routing the magazine from teacher to teacher instead is a much better option.

Assume that your principal says that you are to do as you are told— no questions asked or answered. Now you are in a very sticky situation. You are being asked to do something that you know is illegal, but you are afraid not to do it. You could copy the article as asked, but (5) document the occurrence, so that should some sort of retaliation transpire involving the copyright owners, you would have a record of your stance and actions; (6) place such documentation in your personnel files; (7) contact your teachers' union advocate, explain the situation, and ask for help and advice; (8) contact your school district attorney, inform him or her of the situation and request guidance; and/or (9) contact your professional organization(s) for support on what actions to take.

Other ways to deal with someone who asks you to violate copyright law include (10) encourage correct action; (11) provide examples of infringements and the actions taken against the infringers; (12) supply a copy of those parts of the law of importance in your specific instance; (13) remain composed and empathetic; (14) point out those parts of the work's documentation that list what the copyright owners consider infringement; (15) encourage keeping records of all licenses, permissions, etc.; and (16) remind others that they will be held accountable for what they do (Butler, 2003). It is possible that some educators are simply not aware of how important copyright law is in their world. For example, many educators believe that in a nonprofit educational setting the borrowing of another's works is allowed indiscriminately. This is simply not true, as shown in this book. Therefore, keeping copyright information at the forefront of educators' minds is imperative. Perhaps the best way to achieve compliance with copyright law is to educate—something that teachers and librarians do well.

HOW AND WHY TO TEACH/TRAIN STUDENTS AND OTHERS IN COPYRIGHT LAW

In this society, copyright and other intellectual property issues are not often taught in the schools. For some reason, once you become an adult, it is assumed that you will—by osmosis?—know when you are infringing on an owner's copyright and when you are not, as well as how to tell the difference. Obviously, nothing is further from the truth. Everyone needs to learn about copyright law, and this involves being educated as to its various concepts and issues. A number of universities across the nation offer classes which deal, all or partially, with copyright law, educators, and media.[2] Assuming that a teacher, school library media or technology specialist, or administrator takes such a course, that person could return to his or her school or school district and offer in-services or teacher workshops. Such workshops should ideally occur at the beginning of the school year and involve the administration. The workshop instructor should be prepared to (1) present copyright in terms of ethics; (2) help others work through copyright problems; (3) use as many local examples of violations as possible; (4) have answers ready to promote copyright compliance versus noncompliance; and (5) explain fair use—probably the most important copyright concept for teachers and librarians (Pennock, 1991). Be aware that the Web contains any number of sites that can be used with, and by, teachers and librarians for copyright information (Gummess, 2003; Chausis, 2003; University of Missouri, n.d.; Harper, 2001). Now, what about the students?

Students, elementary through secondary, can also be taught everything from the rudiments of copyright à la the parts of the book[3] (lower elementary) to the extensive copyright information needed to create a viable multimedia presentation (high school). In the case of students, teachers can take it upon themselves to provide a copyright unit to their classes or ask the school library media specialist or technology coordinator to do so. In addition, outside resources, such as the school district's copyright attorney, might be brought in for a presentation to both students and faculty. As the author of this book on copyright for teachers and librarians, I recommend that students begin copyright instruction in elementary school, and that such lessons expand in complexity as students go through the grades up to, and including, their senior year.

Where can teachers find lessons and curricular support with which to teach their students about copyright and related issues, including plagiarism? Any number of units and activities exist in instructional manuals and books (Bacon, 2003; Druse, 1997). In addition, the Internet is a veritable treasure chest of copyright information, including lesson plans and activities aimed at or that can be used with students, grades K-12. Activities on such Web sites range from making copyright Web pages to quizzes and tests to copyright worksheets to an Internet treasure hunt (Agnew, Gummess, Hudson, 2001; Friends of Active Copyright Education, 2001; Columbus Education Association and Otterbein College, 2002; CyberSmart, 2004; Drew, Lagnellier, and Valcik, 2002; Davidson, 2002; Harper, 2001; Madeline and Madeline, 2000; O'Mahoney, 2001; Pappas, 2000). It is important to remember, as you access books and Web sites on copyright, that because copyright is a gray area, not all authors agree. In addition, copyright law may change as new works or formats for works are developed and new ways of using works are created. Because of this, it is also important to be aware of the date of the material you consult; what you seek advice from, ideally, should be as current as is possible. This way, final decisions as to what to present to your classes will be yours. Always look for reputable Internet sites, print sources, and other media of information.

CONCLUSION

Fair use, public domain, permissions, licenses, documentation . . . these copyright terms are found throughout this book; without them, copyright and media usage in the K-12 schools would be a moot point. As can be seen throughout this book, such terms overlap—sometimes one will work while another will not—sometimes two or more will help you as you copy or borrow others' work to support your curriculum and instruct your students. It varies exponentially. I hope that this book will point you, the K-12 teacher and librarian, in the right direction when working with your students, fellow faculty, administrators, and others, as you instruct the next generation of copyright-compliant individuals.

END NOTES

1. Most individual schools or school systems have general policies and procedures focusing on intellectual property concerns and other ethical issues. For example, a school system may have a copyright policy created by the school attorney. In addition, many school media centers, either individually or in conjunction with general school policies, have written collection development guidelines that cover such ethical issues as (a) privacy, (b) piracy, and (c) intellectual freedom, as they relate to copyright. Also, (d) acceptable use policies are common in today's elementary, middle, and secondary schools. Such policies focus on student Internet use and the penalties for when these policies are not met. Privacy, piracy, intellectual freedom, acceptable use policies, and (e) ethics codes are addressed in more detail below.

   (a) Privacy is "information about oneself that is kept from others" (Winter, 1997, 1). The right to privacy is an intrinsic precept of all American citizens, most obviously supported in the First and Fourth Amendments of the Bill of Rights (Mitchell, Message 5). In twenty-first-century America, privacy is very much a concern. It is addressed in terms of medical information, federal acts and bills, libraries, children and families, and the Internet, as well as other areas (Adams, 2000; Kishwaukee Health System, 2003; Mitchell, 2003, Messages 5–10, 12, 13).

   (b) Often defined in terms of software and videos, piracy is essentially the unauthorized copying of a medium for use and sale (World Domination, 1998).

   (c) Intellectual freedom can be defined in two parts: "the right of any person to hold any belief whatever on any subject, and to express such beliefs or ideas in whatever way the person believes appropriate" and "the right of unrestricted access to all information and ideas regardless of the medium of communication used" (ALA Office for Intellectual Freedom, 1989, ix).

(d) Acceptable use policies or AUPs "identify principles of netiquette and stipulate specific guidelines for educational use of network resources" (MacDonald, 1997, 103).

(e) Many professional organizations, whose memberships claim educators, also have ethics policies, procedures, and guidelines (Association for Educational Communications and Technology, 2002; ALA, 2003; National Education Association, 2003).

2. The author of this book, Dr. Rebecca P. Butler, teaches a class on copyright and technology at Northern Illinois University, DeKalb, Illinois.

3. When teaching the parts of a book, the location of the copyright date on the verso (back) of the title page is normally pointed out, as is the symbol for a copyright notice ©.

REFERENCES

Adams, Helen. 2000. "The Internet Invasion: Is Privacy at Risk?" Professional Development Series. McHenry, IL: Follett.

Agnew, Janet, Glen Gummess, and Mike Hudson. 2001. "Copyright Bay." Joliet, IL: University of Saint Francis. Available: www.stfrancis.edu/cid/copyrightbay/ (accessed June 7, 2004).

American Library Association (ALA), Office for Intellectual Freedom. 1989. *Intellectual Freedom Manual*, 3rd ed. Chicago: ALA.

———. 2004. "Code of Ethics of the American Library Association" (adopted by ALA Council June 28, 1995). Chicago: ALA. Available: www.ala.org/ala/oif/statementspols/codeofethics/codeethics.htm (available June 11, 2004).

Association for Educational Communications and Technology. "A Code of Professional Ethics" Bloomington, IN: AECT (October). Available: www.aect.org/Intranet/Publications/ethics/ethics03.html (accessed June 7, 2004).

Bacon, Pamela S. 2003. *100 More Library Lifesavers: A Survival Guide for School Library Media Specialists*. Westport, CT: Libraries Unlimited.

Butler, Rebecca P. 2002. "Software Piracy: Don't Let It Byte You." *Knowledge Quest* 31, no. 2 (November/December): 41–42.

————. 2003. "Copyright Law and Organizing the Internet." *Library Trends* 52, no. 2 (Fall): 307–317.

Chausis, Charlene. 2003. "Copyright Issues in the Classroom" Lincolnshire, IL: Adlai E. Stevenson High School (January). Available: www4.district125.k12.il.us./webmeisters/cchausis/Copyright.html (accessed June 7, 2004).

"Copyright with CyberBee." Columbus [OH] Education Association and Otterbein College. 2002. Available: www.cyberbee.com/copyrt.html (accessed June 7, 2004).

CyberSmart! 2004. [Lesson Plans]. "Considering Copying." CyperSmart School Program and Macmillan McGraw-Hill. Available: www.cybersmartcurriculum.org/lesson_plans/68_09.asp (accessed June 7, 2004).

Davidson, Hall. 2002. "The Educators' Guide to Copyright and Fair Use." *Technology and Learning* 23, no. 3 (October): 26, 28–32.

Drew, Allison, Dia Langellier, and Maggie Valcik. 2002. "FAQ's for Educators on Intellectual Property, Copyright, and Plagiarism." Urbana-Champaign: University of Illinois. (July). Available: http://lrs.ed.uiuc.edu/wp/copyright-2002/indexfaq.html (accessed June 7, 2004).

Druce, Arden. 1997. *Library Lessons for 7–9.* Lanham, MD: Scarecrow.

FA©E Friends of Active Copyright Education. 2001. "Copyright Kids." New York: Copyright Society of the U.S.A. Available: www.csusa.org/face/index.htm (accessed June 7, 2004).

Gummess, Glen. 2003. "Copyright Bay." Joliet, IL: University of St. Francis. (June). Available: www.nmjc.cc.nm.us/copyrightbay/coprbay.htm (accessed June 7, 2004).

Harper, Georgia. 2001. "The UT System Crash Course in Copyright." Austin: University of Texas. Available: www.utsystem.edu/ogc/intellectualproperty/cprtindx.htm (accessed June 7, 2004).

It's Illegal to Violate Copyright Law. 1991. [Video]. 10 min. Frederick, MD: Training Media Association.

JMUWeb Management. 2003. "Copyright for Educators." Harrisonburg, VA. (March 2003). Available: http://falcon.jmu.edu/~ramseyil/copy.htm (accessed June 7, 2004).

Kishwaukee Health System. 2003. "Joint Notice of Privacy Practices." DeKalb, IL: Kishwaukee Health System.

MacDonald, Randall M. 1997. *The Internet and the School Library Media Specialist.* Westport, CT: Greenwood.

Madeline, Kimberly, and Katie Madeline. 2000. "From Pokéman to Picasso, Art Rights and Wrongs: Copyrights." New York: ThinkQuest and the Harry Eichler School. Available: http://library.thinkquest.org/ J001570/Copyrightinfo.html (accessed June 7, 2004).

Mitchell, Kathy. 2003. *The Online Privacy Tutorial* [sent as series of e-mail messages]. Washington, DC: American Library Association, Washington Office.

"Message #5: Constitutional Origin of the Right to Privacy."

"Message #6: Federal Statutory Privacy Law."

"Message #7: Introduction to Children's Online Privacy Protection Act."

"Message #9: Children and Privacy in School Libraries."

"Message #10: Family Educational Rights and Privacy Act."

"Message #12: Law Enforcement and Patron Privacy."

"Message #13: The USA Patriot Act."

National Education Association (NEA). 2003. "Code of Ethics of the Education Profession." Washington, D.C.: NEA. Available: www.nea.org/code.html (accessed June 7, 2004).

O'Mahoney, Benedict. 2004. "Copyright Website." Foster City: Copyright Website LLC. Available: www.benedict.com/ (accessed June 7, 2004).

Pappas, Marjorie. 2002. "Hunt for Copyright Gems." Richmond: Eastern Kentucky University. (November). Available: www.kn.pacbell.com/ wired/fil/pages/huntcopyrighma.html (accessed May 1, 2004).

Pennock, Robin. 1991. "Read My Lips: Copyright." *School Library Journal* 37, no. 6 (June): 50.

University of Missouri at Columbia, College of Education. n.d. "Copyright Law Webquest for Teachers." Available: http://tiger.coe.missouri. edu/~ksgdf/CopyrightWebquest (accessed June 7, 2004).

World Domination. 1998. "Software Piracy: Cause and Consequence (September 21, 1997)." Houston, TX. (January). Available: www.io.com/~pantheon/myWorld/IMHO/essays/piracy.html (accessed June 11, 2004).

Winter, Kenneth A. 1977. "Privacy and the Rights and Responsibilities of Librarians." Greensboro: University of North Carolina. Available: http://alexia.lis.uiuc.edu/review/winter1997/winter.html (accessed June 7, 2004).

Appendices

The following appendices contain selected sections of the U.S. Copyright Law, 1976: Public Law 94-553 (Title 17 of the U.S. Code). These sections contain the more important parts of the law for K-12 educators: the rights of the copyright owner; the fair use provisions; statutory exemptions for libraries, educators, and people with disabilities; copyright ownership provisions; copyright duration; and damages for infringement. For the complete law, see <www.copyright.gov/>.

APPENDIX A

§ 106. Exclusive rights in copyrighted works

Subject to sections 107 through 122, the owner of copyright under this title has the exclusive rights to do and to authorize any of the following:

(1) to reproduce the copyrighted work in copies or phonorecords;

(2) to prepare derivative works based upon the copyrighted work;

(3) to distribute copies or phonorecords of the copyrighted work to the public by sale or other transfer of ownership, or by rental, lease, or lending;

(4) in the case of literary, musical, dramatic, and choreographic works, pantomimes, and motion pictures and other audiovisual works, to perform the copyrighted work publicly;

(5) in the case of literary, musical, dramatic, and choreographic works, pantomimes, and pictorial, graphic, or sculptural works, including the individual images of a motion picture or other audiovisual work, to display the copyrighted work publicly; and

(6) in the case of sound recordings, to perform the copyrighted work publicly by means of a digital audio transmission.

APPENDIX B

§ 107. Limitations on exclusive rights: Fair use

Notwithstanding the provisions of sections 106 and 106A, the fair use of a copyrighted work, including such use by reproduction in copies or phonorecords or by any other means specified by that section, for purposes such as criticism, comment, news reporting, teaching (including multiple copies for classroom use), scholarship, or research, is not an infringement of copyright. In determining whether the use made of a work in any particular case is a fair use the factors to be considered shall include —

(1) the purpose and character of the use, including whether such use is of a commercial nature or is for nonprofit educational purposes;
(2) the nature of the copyrighted work;
(3) the amount and substantiality of the portion used in relation to the copyrighted work as a whole; and
(4) the effect of the use upon the potential market for or value of the copyrighted work.

The fact that a work is unpublished shall not itself bar a finding of fair use if such finding is made upon consideration of all the above factors.

APPENDIX C

§ 108. Limitations on exclusive rights: Reproduction by libraries and archives

(a) Except as otherwise provided in this title and notwithstanding the provisions of section 106, it is not an infringement of copyright for a library or archives, or any of its employees acting within the scope of their employment, to reproduce no more than one copy or phonorecord of a work, except as provided in subsections (b) and (c), or to distribute such copy or phonorecord, under the conditions specified by this section, if —

(1)   the reproduction or distribution is made without any purpose of direct or indirect commercial advantage;

(2)   the collections of the library or archives are (i) open to the public, or (ii) available not only to researchers affiliated with the library or archives or with the institution of which it is a part, but also to other persons doing research in a specialized field; and

(3)   the reproduction or distribution of the work includes a notice of copyright that appears on the copy or phonorecord that is reproduced under the provisions of this section, or includes a legend stating that the work may be protected by copyright if no such notice can be found on the copy or phonorecord that is reproduced under the provisions of this section.

(b) The rights of reproduction and distribution under this section apply to three copies or phonorecords of an unpublished work duplicated solely for purposes of preservation and security or for deposit for research use in another library or archives of the type described by clause (2) of subsection (a), if —

(1)   the copy or phonorecord reproduced is currently in the collections of the library or archives; and

(2)   any such copy or phonorecord that is reproduced in digital format is not otherwise distributed in that format and is not made available to the public in that format outside the premises of the library or archives.

(c) The right of reproduction under this section applies to three copies or phonorecords of a published work duplicated solely for the purpose of replacement of a copy or phonorecord that is damaged, deteriorating, lost, or stolen, or if the existing format in which the work is stored has become obsolete, if —

(1) the library or archives has, after a reasonable effort, determined that an unused replacement cannot be obtained at a fair price; and

(2) any such copy or phonorecord that is reproduced in digital format is not made available to the public in that format outside the premises of the library or archives in lawful possession of such copy.

For purposes of this subsection, a format shall be considered obsolete if the machine or device necessary to render perceptible a work stored in that format is no longer manufactured or is no longer reasonably available in the commercial marketplace.

(d) The rights of reproduction and distribution under this section apply to a copy, made from the collection of a library or archives where the user makes his or her request or from that of another library or archives, of no more than one article or other contribution to a copyrighted collection or periodical issue, or to a copy or phonorecord of a small part of any other copyrighted work, if —

(1) the copy or phonorecord becomes the property of the user, and the library or archives has had no notice that the copy or phonorecord would be used for any purpose other than private study, scholarship, or research; and

(2) the library or archives displays prominently, at the place where orders are accepted, and includes on its order form, a warning of copyright in accordance with requirements that the Register of Copyrights shall prescribe by regulation.

(e) The rights of reproduction and distribution under this section apply to the entire work, or to a substantial part of it, made from the collection of a library or archives where the user makes his or her request or from that of another library or archives, if the library or archives has first determined, on the basis of a reasonable investigation, that a copy or phonorecord of the copyrighted work cannot be obtained at a fair price, if —

(1) the copy or phonorecord becomes the property of the user, and the library or archives has had no notice that the copy or phonorecord would be used for any purpose other than private study, scholarship, or research; and

(2)   the library or archives displays prominently, at the place where orders are accepted, and includes on its order form, a warning of copyright in accordance with requirements that the Register of Copyrights shall prescribe by regulation.

(f) Nothing in this section —

(1)   shall be construed to impose liability for copyright infringement upon a library or archives or its employees for the unsupervised use of reproducing equipment located on its premises: *Provided*, That such equipment displays a notice that the making of a copy may be subject to the copyright law;

(2)   excuses a person who uses such reproducing equipment or who requests a copy or phonorecord under subsection (d) from liability for copyright infringement for any such act, or for any later use of such copy or phonorecord, if it exceeds fair use as provided by section 107;

(3)   shall be construed to limit the reproduction and distribution by lending of a limited number of copies and excerpts by a library or archives of an audiovisual news program, subject to clauses (1), (2), and (3) of subsection (a); or

(4)   in any way affects the right of fair use as provided by section 107, or any contractual obligations assumed at any time by the library or archives when it obtained a copy or phonorecord of a work in its collections.

(g) The rights of reproduction and distribution under this section extend to the isolated and unrelated reproduction or distribution of a single copy or phonorecord of the same material on separate occasions, but do not extend to cases where the library or archives, or its employee —

(1)   is aware or has substantial reason to believe that it is engaging in the related or concerted reproduction or distribution of multiple copies or phonorecords of the same material, whether made on one occasion or over a period of time, and whether intended for aggregate use by one or more individuals or for separate use by the individual members of a group; or

(2)   engages in the systematic reproduction or distribution of single or multiple copies or phonorecords of material described in subsection (d): *Provided*, That nothing in this clause prevents a library or archives from participating in interlibrary arrangements that do not

have, as their purpose or effect, that the library or archives receiving such copies or phonorecords for distribution does so in such aggregate quantities as to substitute for a subscription to or purchase of such work.

(h)(1) For purposes of this section, during the last 20 years of any term of copyright of a published work, a library or archives, including a nonprofit educational institution that functions as such, may reproduce, distribute, display, or perform in facsimile or digital form a copy or phonorecord of such work, or portions thereof, for purposes of preservation, scholarship, or research, if such library or archives has first determined, on the basis of a reasonable investigation, that none of the conditions set forth in subparagraphs (A), (B), and (C) of paragraph (2) apply.
(2) No reproduction, distribution, display, or performance is authorized under this subsection if —

(A) the work is subject to normal commercial exploitation;
(B) a copy or phonorecord of the work can be obtained at a reasonable price; or
(C) the copyright owner or its agent provides notice pursuant to regulations promulgated by the Register of Copyrights that either of the conditions set forth in subparagraphs (A) and (B) applies.
(3) The exemption provided in this subsection does not apply to any subsequent uses by users other than such library or archives.
(i) The rights of reproduction and distribution under this section do not apply to a musical work, a pictorial, graphic or sculptural work, or a motion picture or other audiovisual work other than an audiovisual work dealing with news, except that no such limitation shall apply with respect to rights granted by subsections (b) and (c), or with respect to pictorial or graphic works published as illustrations, diagrams, or similar adjuncts to works of which copies are reproduced or distributed in accordance with subsections (d) and (e).

APPENDIX D

§ 110. Limitations on exclusive rights: Exemption of certain performances and displays

Notwithstanding the provisions of section 106, the following are not infringements of copyright:

(1) performance or display of a work by instructors or pupils in the course of face-to-face teaching activities of a nonprofit educational institution, in a classroom or similar place devoted to instruction, unless, in the case of a motion picture or other audiovisual work, the performance, or the display of individual images, is given by means of a copy that was not lawfully made under this title, and that the person responsible for the performance knew or had reason to believe was not lawfully made;

(2) except with respect to a work produced or marketed primarily for performance or display as part of mediated instructional activities transmitted via digital networks, or a performance or display that is given by means of a copy or phonorecord that is not lawfully made and acquired under this title, and the transmitting government body or accredited nonprofit educational institution knew or had reason to believe was not lawfully made and acquired, the performance of a nondramatic literary or musical work or reasonable and limited portions of any other work, or display of a work in an amount comparable to that which is typically displayed in the course of a live classroom session, by or in the course of a transmission, if —

(A) the performance or display is made by, at the direction of, or under the actual supervision of an instructor as an integral part of a class session offered as a regular part of the systematic mediated instructional activities of a governmental body or an accredited nonprofit educational institution;

(B) the performance or display is directly related and of material assistance to the teaching content of the transmission;

(C) the transmission is made solely for, and, to the extent technologically feasible, the reception of such transmission is limited to —

(i) students officially enrolled in the course for which the transmission is made; or

(ii) officers or employees of governmental bodies as a part of their official duties or employment; and

(D) the transmitting body or institution —

(i)   institutes policies regarding copyright, provides informational materials to faculty, students, and relevant staff members that accurately describe, and promote compliance with, the laws of the United States relating to copyright, and provides notice to students that materials used in connection with the course may be subject to copyright protection; and

(ii) in the case of digital transmissions —

(I)   applies technological measures that reasonably prevent —

(aa) retention of the work in accessible form by recipients of the transmission from the transmitting body or institution for longer than the class session; and

(bb) unauthorized further dissemination of the work in accessible form by such recipients to others; and

(II) does not engage in conduct that could reasonably be expected to interfere with technological measures used by copyright owners to prevent such retention or unauthorized further dissemination;

(3) performance of a nondramatic literary or musical work or of a dramatico-musical work of a religious nature, or display of a work, in the course of services at a place of worship or other religious assembly;

(4) performance of a nondramatic literary or musical work otherwise than in a transmission to the public, without any purpose of direct or indirect commercial advantage and without payment of any fee or other compensation for the performance to any of its performers, promoters, or organizers, if —

(A) there is no direct or indirect admission charge; or

(B) the proceeds, after deducting the reasonable costs of producing the performance, are used exclusively for educational, religious, or charitable purposes and not for private financial gain, except where the copyright owner has served notice of objection to the performance under the following conditions:

(i)   the notice shall be in writing and signed by the copyright owner or such owner's duly authorized agent; and

(ii) the notice shall be served on the person responsible for the performance at least seven days before the date of the performance, and shall state the reasons for the objection; and

(iii) the notice shall comply, in form, content, and manner of service, with requirements that the Register of Copyrights shall prescribe by regulation;

(5)(A) except as provided in subparagraph (B), communication of a transmission embodying a performance or display of a work by the public reception of the transmission on a single receiving apparatus of a kind commonly used in private homes, unless —

(i)   a direct charge is made to see or hear the transmission; or

(ii) the transmission thus received is further transmitted to the public;

(B) communication by an establishment of a transmission or retransmission embodying a performance or display of a nondramatic musical work intended to be received by the general public, originated by a radio or television broadcast station licensed as such by the Federal Communications Commission, or, if an audiovisual transmission, by a cable system or satellite carrier, if —

(i)   in the case of an establishment other than a food service or drinking establishment, either the establishment in which the communication occurs has less than 2,000 gross square feet of space (excluding space used for customer parking and for no other purpose), or the establishment in which the communication occurs has 2,000 or more gross square feet of space (excluding space used for customer parking and for no other purpose) and —

(I)   if the performance is by audio means only, the performance is communicated by means of a total of not more than 6 loudspeakers, of which not more than 4 loudspeakers are located in any 1 room or adjoining outdoor space; or

(II) if the performance or display is by audiovisual means, any visual portion of the performance or display is communicated by means of a total of not more than 4 audiovisual devices, of which not more than 1 audiovisual device is located in any 1 room, and no such audiovisual device has a diagonal screen size greater than 55 inches, and any audio portion of the performance or display is communicated by means of a total of not more than 6 loudspeakers, of which not more than 4 loudspeakers are located in any 1 room or adjoining outdoor space;

(ii) in the case of a food service or drinking establishment, either the establishment in which the communication occurs has less than 3,750 gross square feet of space (excluding space used for customer parking and for no other purpose), or the establishment in which the communication occurs has 3,750 gross square feet of space or more (excluding space used for customer parking and for no other purpose) and —

(I) if the performance is by audio means only, the performance is communicated by means of a total of not more than 6 loudspeakers, of which not more than 4 loudspeakers are located in any 1 room or adjoining outdoor space; or

(II) if the performance or display is by audiovisual means, any visual portion of the performance or display is communicated by means of a total of not more than 4 audiovisual devices, of which not more than 1 audiovisual device is located in any 1 room, and no such audiovisual device has a diagonal screen size greater than 55 inches, and any audio portion of the performance or display is communicated by means of a total of not more than 6 loudspeakers, of which not more than 4 loudspeakers are located in any 1 room or adjoining outdoor space;

(iii) no direct charge is made to see or hear the transmission or retransmission;

(iv) the transmission or retransmission is not further transmitted beyond the establishment where it is received; and

(v) the transmission or retransmission is licensed by the copyright owner of the work so publicly performed or displayed;

(6) performance of a nondramatic musical work by a governmental body or a nonprofit agricultural or horticultural organization, in the course of an annual agricultural or horticultural fair or exhibition conducted by such body or organization; the exemption provided by this clause shall extend to any liability for copyright infringement that would otherwise be imposed on such body or organization, under doctrines of vicarious liability or related infringement, for a performance by a concessionnaire, business establishment, or other person at such fair or exhibition, but shall not excuse any such person from liability for the performance;

(7) performance of a nondramatic musical work by a vending establishment open to the public at large without any direct or indirect admission charge, where the sole purpose of the performance is to promote the retail sale of copies or phonorecords of the work, or of the audiovisual or other devices utilized in such performance, and the performance is not transmitted beyond the place where the establishment is located and is within the immediate area where the sale is occurring;

(8) performance of a nondramatic literary work, by or in the course of a transmission specifically designed for and primarily directed to blind or other handicapped persons who are unable to read nor-

mal printed material as a result of their handicap, or deaf or other handicapped persons who are unable to hear the aural signals accompanying a transmission of visual signals, if the performance is made without any purpose of direct or indirect commercial advantage and its transmission is made through the facilities of: (i) a governmental body; or (ii) a noncommercial educational broadcast station (as defined in section 397 of title 47); or (iii) a radio subcarrier authorization (as defined in 47 CFR 73.293–73.295 and 73.593–73.595); or (iv) a cable system (as defined in section 111 (f));

(9)   performance on a single occasion of a dramatic literary work published at least ten years before the date of the performance, by or in the course of a transmission specifically designed for and primarily directed to blind or other handicapped persons who are unable to read normal printed material as a result of their handicap, if the performance is made without any purpose of direct or indirect commercial advantage and its transmission is made through the facilities of a radio subcarrier authorization referred to in clause (8) (iii), *Provided,* That the provisions of this clause shall not be applicable to more than one performance of the same work by the same performers or under the auspices of the same organization; and

(10)   notwithstanding paragraph (4), the following is not an infringement of copyright: performance of a nondramatic literary or musical work in the course of a social function which is organized and promoted by a nonprofit veterans' organization or a nonprofit fraternal organization to which the general public is not invited, but not including the invitees of the organizations, if the proceeds from the performance, after deducting the reasonable costs of producing the performance, are used exclusively for charitable purposes and not for financial gain. For purposes of this section the social functions of any college or university fraternity or sorority shall not be included unless the social function is held solely to raise funds for a specific charitable purpose.

The exemptions provided under paragraph (5) shall not be taken into account in any administrative, judicial, or other governmental proceeding to set or adjust the royalties payable to copyright owners for the public performance or display of their works. Royalties payable to copyright owners for any public performance or display of their works other than such performances or displays as are exempted under paragraph (5) shall not be diminished in any respect as a result of such exemption.

In paragraph (2), the term "mediated instructional activities" with respect to the performance or display of a work by digital transmission under this section refers to activities that use such work as an integral part of the class experience, controlled by or under the actual supervision of the instructor and analogous to the type of performance or display that would take place in a live classroom setting. The term does not refer to activities that use, in 1 or more class sessions of a single course, such works as textbooks, course packs, or other material in any media, copies or phonorecords of which are typically purchased or acquired by the students in higher education for their independent use and retention or are typically purchased or acquired for elementary and secondary students for their possession and independent use.

For purposes of paragraph (2), accreditation —

(A)   with respect to an institution providing post-secondary education, shall be as determined by a regional or national accrediting agency recognized by the Council on Higher Education Accreditation or the United States Department of Education; and

(B)   with respect to an institution providing elementary or secondary education, shall be as recognized by the applicable state certification or licensing procedures.

For purposes of paragraph (2), no governmental body or accredited non-profit educational institution shall be liable for infringement by reason of the transient or temporary storage of material carried out through the automatic technical process of a digital transmission of the performance or display of that material as authorized under paragraph (2). No such material stored on the system or network controlled or operated by the transmitting body or institution under this paragraph shall be maintained on such system or network in a manner ordinarily accessible to anyone other than anticipated recipients. No such copy shall be maintained on the system or network in a manner ordinarily accessible to such anticipated recipients for a longer period than is reasonably necessary to facilitate the transmissions for which it was made.

APPENDIX E

§ 121. Limitations on exclusive rights: reproduction for blind or other people with disabilities

(a) Notwithstanding the provisions of section 106, it is not an infringement of copyright for an authorized entity to reproduce or to distribute copies or phonorecords of a previously published, nondramatic literary work if such copies or phonorecords are reproduced or distributed in specialized formats exclusively for use by blind or other persons with disabilities.

(b)(1) Copies or phonorecords to which this section applies shall —

(A) not be reproduced or distributed in a format other than a specialized format exclusively for use by blind or other persons with disabilities;

(B) bear a notice that any further reproduction or distribution in a format other than a specialized format is an infringement; and

(C) include a copyright notice identifying the copyright owner and the date of the original publication.

(2) The provisions of this subsection shall not apply to standardized, secure, or norm-referenced tests and related testing material, or to computer programs, except the portions thereof that are in conventional human language (including descriptions of pictorial works) and displayed to users in the ordinary course of using the computer programs.

(c) For purposes of this section, the term —

(1) "authorized entity" means a nonprofit organization or a governmental agency that has a primary mission to provide specialized services relating to training, education, or adaptive reading or information access needs of blind or other persons with disabilities;

(2) "blind or other persons with disabilities" means individuals who are eligible or who may qualify in accordance with the Act entitled "An Act to provide books for the adult blind", approved March 3, 1931 (2 U.S.C. 135a; 46 Stat. 1487) to receive books and other publications produced in specialized formats; and

(3) "specialized formats" means braille, audio, or digital text which is exclusively for use by blind or other persons with disabilities.

APPENDIX F

§ 201. Ownership of copyright

(a) Initial Ownership. — Copyright in a work protected under this title vests initially in the author or authors of the work. The authors of a joint work are coowner of copyright in the work.

(b) Works Made for Hire. — In the case of a work made for hire, the employer or other person for whom the work was prepared is considered the author for purposes of this title, and, unless the parties have expressly agreed otherwise in a written instrument signed by them, owns all of the rights comprised in the copyright.

(c) Contributions to Collective Works. — Copyright in each separate contribution to a collective work is distinct from copyright in the collective work as a whole, and vests initially in the author of the contribution. In the absence of an express transfer of the copyright or of any rights under it, the owner of copyright in the collective work is presumed to have acquired only the privilege of reproducing and distributing the contribution as part of that particular collective work, any revision of that collective work, and any later collective work in the same series.

(d) Transfer of Ownership. —

 (1) The ownership of a copyright may be transferred in whole or in part by any means of conveyance or by operation of law, and may be bequeathed by will or pass as personal property by the applicable laws of intestate succession.

 (2) Any of the exclusive rights comprised in a copyright, including any subdivision of any of the rights specified by section 106, may be transferred as provided by clause (1) and owned separately. The owner of any particular exclusive right is entitled, to the extent of that right, to all of the protection and remedies accorded to the copyright owner by this title.

(e) Involuntary Transfer. — When an individual author's ownership of a copyright, or of any of the exclusive rights under a copyright, has not previously been transferred voluntarily by that individual author, no action by any governmental body or other official or organization purporting to seize, expropriate, transfer, or exercise rights of ownership with respect to the copyright, or any of the exclusive rights under a copyright, shall be given effect under this title, except as provided under title 11.

APPENDIX G

§ 302. Duration of copyright: Works created on or after January 1, 1978

(a)   In General. — Copyright in a work created on or after January 1, 1978, subsists from its creation and, except as provided by the following subsections, endures for a term consisting of the life of the author and 70 years after the author's death.

(b)   Joint Works. — In the case of a joint work prepared by two or more authors who did not work for hire, the copyright endures for a term consisting of the life of the last surviving author and 70 years after such last surviving author's death.

(c)   Anonymous Works, Pseudonymous Works, and Works Made for Hire. — In the case of an anonymous work, a pseudonymous work, or a work made for hire, the copyright endures for a term of 95 years from the year of its first publication, or a term of 120 years from the year of its creation, whichever expires first. If, before the end of such term, the identity of one or more of the authors of an anonymous or pseudonymous work is revealed in the records of a registration made for that work under subsections (a) or (d) of section 408, or in the records provided by this subsection, the copyright in the work endures for the term specified by subsection (a) or (b), based on the life of the author or authors whose identity has been revealed. Any person having an interest in the copyright in an anonymous or pseudonymous work may at any time record, in records to be maintained by the Copyright Office for that purpose, a statement identifying one or more authors of the work; the statement shall also identify the person filing it, the nature of that person's interest, the source of the information recorded, and the particular work affected, and shall comply in form and content with requirements that the Register of Copyrights shall prescribe by regulation.

(d)   Records Relating to Death of Authors. — Any person having an interest in a copyright may at any time record in the Copyright Office a statement of the date of death of the author of the copyrighted work, or a statement that the author is still living on a particular date. The statement shall identify the person filing it, the nature of that person's interest, and the source of the information recorded, and shall comply in form and content with requirements that the Register of Copyrights shall prescribe by regulation. The Register shall maintain current records of information relating to the death of authors of copyrighted works, based on such recorded statements and, to the extent the Register considers practicable, on data contained in any of the records of the Copyright Office or in other reference sources.

(e) Presumption as to Author's Death. — After a period of 95 years from the year of first publication of a work, or a period of 120 years from the year of its creation, whichever expires first, any person who obtains from the Copyright Office a certified report that the records provided by subsection (d) disclose nothing to indicate that the author of the work is living, or died less than 70 years before, is entitled to the benefit of a presumption that the author has been dead for at least 70 years. Reliance in good faith upon this presumption shall be a complete defense to any action for infringement under this title.

APPENDIX H

§ 504. Remedies for infringement: Damages and profits

(a)   In General. — Except as otherwise provided by this title, an infringer of copyright is liable for either —

   (1)   the copyright owner's actual damages and any additional profits of the infringer, as provided by subsection (b); or

   (2)   statutory damages, as provided by subsection (c).

(b)   Actual Damages and Profits. — The copyright owner is entitled to recover the actual damages suffered by him or her as a result of the infringement, and any profits of the infringer that are attributable to the infringement and are not taken into account in computing the actual damages. In establishing the infringer's profits, the copyright owner is required to present proof only of the infringer's gross revenue, and the infringer is required to prove his or her deductible expenses and the elements of profit attributable to factors other than the copyrighted work.

(c)   Statutory Damages. —

   (1)   Except as provided by clause (2) of this subsection, the copyright owner may elect, at any time before final judgment is rendered, to recover, instead of actual damages and profits, an award of statutory damages for all infringements involved in the action, with respect to any one work, for which any one infringer is liable individually, or for which any two or more infringers are liable jointly and severally, in a sum of not less than $750 or more than $30,000 as the court considers just. For the purposes of this subsection, all the parts of a compilation or derivative work constitute one work.

   (2)   In a case where the copyright owner sustains the burden of proving, and the court finds, that infringement was committed willfully, the court in its discretion may increase the award of statutory damages to a sum of not more than $150,000. In a case where the infringer sustains the burden of proving, and the court finds, that such infringer was not aware and had no reason to believe that his or her acts constituted an infringement of copyright, the court in its discretion may reduce the award of statutory damages to a sum of not less than $200. The court shall remit statutory damages in any case where an infringer believed and had reasonable grounds for believing that his or her use of the copyrighted work was a fair use under section 107, if the infringer was: (i) an employee or agent of a nonprofit educational

institution, library, or archives acting within the scope of his or her employment who, or such institution, library, or archives itself, which infringed by reproducing the work in copies or phonorecords; or (ii) a public broadcasting entity which or a person who, as a regular part of the nonprofit activities of a public broadcasting entity (as defined in subsection (g) of section 118) infringed by performing a published nondramatic literary work or by reproducing a transmission program embodying a performance of such a work.

(d) Additional Damages in Certain Cases. — In any case in which the court finds that a defendant proprietor of an establishment who claims as a defense that its activities were exempt under section 110(5) did not have reasonable grounds to believe that its use of a copyrighted work was exempt under such section, the plaintiff shall be entitled to, in addition to any award of damages under this section, an additional award of two times the amount of the license fee that the proprietor of the establishment concerned should have paid the plaintiff for such use during the preceding period of up to 3 years.

Index

Flowchart titles are bolded.

About the Author

Rebecca P. Butler is currently an associate professor in the Educational Technology, Research, and Assessment Department in the College of Education at Northern Illinois University (NIU) DeKalb, Illinois. At NIU, she teaches graduate (master's and doctoral) classes in school library media and instructional technology. Prior to moving to NIU in 1998, she was an assistant professor in the Department of Curriculum and Instruction at East Tennessee State University (ETSU). While a faculty member at NIU and ETSU, she has conducted a variety of workshops, conferences, and graduate classes on the topic of copyright. Although the majority have been geared for K-12 teachers and school library media specialists, she has also done numerous presentations on the subject for faculty and staff in various departments at both universities. Dr. Butler also writes a regular column on copyright issues for *Knowledge Quest,* the journal of the American Association of School Librarians (AASL).

Dr. Butler earned a B.A. in library science from the University of Northern Iowa in 1972; an M.S.L.S. from the University of Kentucky in 1978; and a Ph.D. in educational technology/curriculum and instruction from the University of Wisconsin-Madison in 1995. She has worked in a variety of library positions, including several years as a school librarian and library media specialist in public schools (K-12) in Fort Dodge, Dubuque, and Scott County, Iowa, and in a private school in Caracas, Venezuela; as a reference and young adult public librarian in Naperville, Illinois; as a medical librarian in Aurora, Illinois; and as a historian/special librarian in Coshocton, Ohio. During her career as a librarian and educator, Dr. Butler has been an active member in a number of professional organizations, including the American Library Association (ALA), the American Association of School Librarians (AASL), the Association for Educational Communications and Technology, the Illinois School

Library Media Association, the Tennessee Library Association (TLA), the American Educational Research Association, the Freedom to Read Foundation, the International Association of School Librarianship, the International Visual Literacy Association, the Cooperative Children's Book Center, and the Wisconsin Educational Media Association. In these organizations she has served on a variety of committees including the Ad Hoc Task Force on Restrictions on Access to Government Information (ALA); the AASL National Conference Evaluation Committee; the AASL/SIRS Intellectual Freedom Award Committee; the Internet, Libraries and the First Amendment Regional Committee (ALA); as an executive board member of the Tennessee Library Association; and as Co-Chair of the (TLA) Intellectual Freedom Committee. She also served as a planning committee member for the 2001 Conference on Copyright and Intellectual Property Issues for Online Instruction, Northern Illinois University.